AN ACCIDENTAL DISSIDENT

Life and times of a Christian in Communist Romania

Ioan Mihai Oara

ISBN-13 978-0692180877

AN ACCIDENTAL DISSIDENT

Contents

AN ACCIDENTAL DISSIDENT

Introduction

On a spring day, in 1979, after attending an Astronomy lecture, I came out of the old University of Bucharest building, and turned right on the Eduard Quinet Street, going to the University Plaza to catch a bus home. I was only seconds away from a long-expected confrontation with the Securitate, the secret police of the Communist Romania.

At that time in my life I was living in three worlds, with a different role in each one. The first was my immediate young family. I was married for two years with Ana and we had a newborn son, Ruben. This was a world of domestic tranquility and love, in which I was a happy husband and father. We had many friends and a beautiful apartment in walking distance to the center of the city, not far from the University of Bucharest, where I was a student in my fourth year.

The second world was that of mathematics, for which I had both passion and talent. I had discovered my interest in math when I was twelve years old and pursued it ever since, hoping to become a mathematician. This was a fascinating world, filled with exotic landscapes, paradoxes,

4

riddles and beauty. I perceived it as a complicated temple, with infinite details and hidden places which I was contemplating and trying to penetrate deeper and deeper. There were large porticoes which many could see, but also locked doors which I struggled to open. When a new door opened, I was filled with a feeling of euphoria and a desire to go even further.

The third world was that of my newly discovered Christian faith, which provided me with a meaning of life and a relationship to a Higher Being. I was an active member of one of the Baptist churches in Bucharest, where I was leading study groups and even preached occasionally. When pastors or preachers or missionaries arrived from the West, mainly from United States and Great Britain, I was the one who interpreted for them, both in private meetings and when they preached from the pulpit. Most important, I was involved in multiple activities beyond the church itself, which had to be kept secret as they were viewed unfavorably by the Communist Regime. These included secret theological schools, smuggling of Christian literature, and relationships with other dissident groups, both religious and political.

As I started to walk towards the bus stop, I noticed three men standing on the sidewalk, who seemed to be somehow out of place, but I did not pay too much attention to them. They were forming a triangle with an open base towards me. A Dacia car, the ubiquitous Romanian automobile, was stationed on the street next to them. When I was exactly in the center of the triangle, two of them grabbed my hands, while the third opened the back door of the car. They pushed me inside and closed the doors, and then the car took off.

I was surprised only for a few seconds. While it might have looked like a Mafia kidnapping, I was not worried: Bucharest was a civilized city, and I was not aware of any Mafia. I realized that it was the Securitate, the Romanian secret police, the guardian of the Communist state. I did not protest, and I did not ask questions. My kidnappers were also quiet, except some casual conversations, like "Take that street, it has lighter traffic."

Realizing what was happening, my mind started to race with an overwhelming question: What was the immediate reason for my detention? Was it my meeting with an American last week? Was it a transport of books in which I was involved a few weeks before? Was it the fact that I had passed some dissident's messages to the American Embassy? I had to know what they knew, so I could defend myself.

After fifteen minutes, the car pulled in front of the modern building of a district police station. They took me out and escorted me inside. People were coming and going through the lobbies, and after a small wait they took me to a large room with a table in the center and small offices on the sides. I was told to sit at the table, and after a few minutes a young man, around thirty years old, came and sat opposite of me.

What was the offence for which they detained me? That was the question.

The young man introduced himself as a Securitate lieutenant and then asked,

"Why do you think we brought you here?"

I knew better than to answer that question.

***

In persecutionem veritas. In persecution is the truth.
This is my variation of the famous Latin observation: *In vino veritas*. The wine weakens the inhibitions and shows the hidden crevices of one's personality. He may swear and attack his companions, or he will start kissing them and show unusual generosity. Oppression or persecution inhibits normal or superficial behaviors, showing only the dominant traits. He may become a monster or a sycophant, or he may become a fighter against the evil, in secret or in the open.

I was born and raised in the Communist country of Romania. As a child, as a teenager and as a young man, I was confronted with a repressive regime and I struggled to keep my dignity and freedom in the middle of forces which were pushing me to conform to an ideology which I despised.

The twentieth century was one of two grand ideologies: Nazism and Communism. Both claimed some messianic role and endeavored to push humanity towards a new era. Nazism believed in the superiority of the Aryan nations and attempted to build a society in which the superior humans would become masters, eliminating the inferior or using them to their advantage. Communism believed in the inescapable advance of history towards a classless society, without exploitation, in which everyone works and gives according to his or her ability and receives according to his or her needs. It announced the coming of an era of freedom and prosperity. The guillotine of the

French Revolution, the execution squads, the Siberian gulags or the Romanian prisons were supposed to be only temporary instruments used to purge humanity and rush in the new happy era. Both Nazism and Communism grew out of some real injustice and pain, like the suffering of the poor proletarians living in abject conditions in the 19th century in England, or the humiliation of the German nation treated harshly by the victors of the First World War. Both ideologies were picked up by the real gangsters, who took the mantle of leadership and evolved from sacrificing heroes and fighters into tyrannical masters.

Ideologies create passions and forces which tend to unite some people, but also storms which destroy those who do not to join or conform. Such people must find coping strategies to survive. As a prism splits the apparent white light into many colors, the persecution of those who do not conform splits men and women into separate categories. In a free society, most people are similar: they go to work, talk with their friends and neighbors and are relatively moral. They are friendly and polite to each other. Under persecution, they separate: some become loyalists, enjoying the social and economic benefits provided by the regime, some hide, some avoid trouble, and some fight. You will recognize some of these figures in this story, in which I myself traversed some of these categories.

The classic movie Casablanca shows a microcosm of the same type of characters whom I have encountered under the Communist regime. The Nazis are the occupiers who took over the country and repressed any opposition. Rick Blain, played by Humphrey Bogart, despises the Nazis, but is self-absorbed and cynical, refusing to take any side, but later he becomes idealistic and takes risks. Victor Laszlo is a courageous anti-Nazi fighter, once imprisoned by his enemies, but who continues his fight after his escape. Captain Claude Rains is unscrupulous, siding with whoever has the power, but later shows traces of humanity and courage, even saving his friend Rick. Major Heinrich Strasser is the quintessential Nazi, using his power to suppress any sign of opposition. Senior Ferrari only cares for his business, regardless of who is in charge. The newlywed Brandels have only one dream, to escape Casablanca and go to America. If all these people lived thirty years after the war in some nice French town, they would have been good friends, played cards in the evenings and watched soccer games together on TV. The Believer

The Believers are the ones who accept the ideology with all their souls, hearts and minds. Some are the very leaders who impose their ideology on the rest of the society: Hitler, Stalin, Robespierre, Trotsky. If not already at the top, they raise higher and higher, proving themselves reliable to their masters. They form the second and third echelons of power and achieve high positions in the state. Some are fanatics, like Goebbels, who preferred to kill his own children rather than see them grow in a world without Nazism.

Surprisingly, in the 60s and 70s under the Communist regime in Romania, I did not meet people in this category. The Nazis had their true believers, so had the Bolsheviks, but in the 1970s there were few Romanians who believed in Communism. Yes, people of power expressed allegiance to Communism, but few really believed. In private, they either showed doubts or switched beliefs according to the interests of the moment.

The Chameleon

As in the famous novel 1984, occasionally the Power makes sudden changes in the official doctrines, most often because of some immediate personal interests. In the 60s, the Yugoslav leader Tito was reviled by the Communist Party in Romania, who slavishly followed directions from Moscow. In the 70s, Tito became a great leader, a great Communist and a friend of Romania. The same people who attacked him yesterday were now praising him, without any shame for their sudden change.

I saw this chameleonic change at its worst in 1990, when the Communist regime fell. Some local Party leader sang praises to Ceaușescu in November 1989 and sent dissenters into the hands of the Secret Police. However, at the end of December 1989, when the Ceaușescu regime collapsed, he declared himself a freedom lover and a secret fighter against Communism. In the following year, he became a businessman and fired as many people as needed to make it profitable and later became a millionaire.

The Scared Conformist

I met people who did their utmost to conform to the Communist Party line and lived in constant fear not to somehow be perceived as deviating from it. One found out that the Securitate was asking his friend about him and spent sleepless nights worrying. Paradoxically, some of the conformists I met displayed physical courage, much more than what I was capable of. They were dared to climb a rock or to get into a physical fight but had no spine when confronted by authorities.

Many police informers were Scared Conformists. They were asked to report what their friends were saying or doing, and any moral qualms were suppressed by their constant fear.

The Adapter

The Adapter conforms to the ideology externally but opposes it whenever he or she can. Unlike the Chameleon, the Adapter does not show zeal, but does what it takes to insure survival. In the movie Casablanca, the prototype of the Adapter is Captain Louis Renault, who appears to cooperate with the German masters and does nothing to endanger himself by expressing contrary opinions, but secretly and occasionally opposes them. The Adapter is not immoral or amoral, but prudent and shrewd. He is a survivor.

Under Communism I saw many Adapters. A police officer slaps a political suspect, only to protect him from a real beating. A Communist Party member baptizes her children in secret. A teacher reads her students some article about atheism, but then lets them leave a little earlier so they can catch a church service.

The Fighter

The Fighter is opposing the power either openly or in secret, using subversive methods. He is dedicated to the cause of freedom and ready to sacrifice his life for it. This is the Victor Laslo, whose fight is his *reason d'etre*.

I met many Fighters in my days in Communist Romania. Some suffered years of imprisonment in the 50s, a period of maximum repression when the Communist regime attempted to break all traditional economic and political realities of the country and take full control of Romanian society. Some were beaten or tortured and came out of prison with a broken body, but an even stronger fighting spirit. You will encounter some of them in this narrative.

***

Although I write here about times and situations which are not familiar to my readers, I still hope they may find some relevance for their lives. Some problems which we had at a political level back under Communism, reappear constantly in all societies, sometimes in the microcosm of corporations, where one may encounter hypocrisy, exploitation and sycophancy.

There are of course good corporations, faithful to their employees and clients. In hard times, they may tighten the belt and reduce some of the benefits, but overall, they spread the sacrifice evenly and struggle to serve their clients at the highest level of quality possible. Unfortunately, this is not always the case. One of the common manifestations of hypocrisy comes from the companies that declare that their highest priority is the welfare of their employees, while in fact treating them as a cheap commodity.

My wife was once working for a large national retail firm. The CEO declared himself a defender of women's interests and organized yearly galas dedicated to the promotion of women, at which famous or influential people were invited. Despite these declared lofty ideals, in a tight year he fired more than ten thousand workers, the majority women, while he enjoyed a record bonus. This reminded me of how Ceauşescu reduced the country consumption by exporting everything possible, depriving Romanian citizens of some basic needs and forcing them to spend all their free time waiting in food lines. All this happened while the Communist Party declared that its goal is the welfare and prosperity for the people and official propaganda claimed that Romanian citizens live in the most humane and free society in history.

At the store in which my wife was working, there were weekly meetings in which the previous week's sales results were announced. When the store manager announced that sales goals were not only achieved but surpassed, all people in the meeting broke into enthusiastic applause. It was fake, as most of them were paid at close to minimum wage and the company record sales had zero influence on their income. This reminded me of the political meetings in Romania, at which somebody delivered a speech about the great success of Communism and about the wisdom of our leader, and everybody applauded with a fake enthusiasm. Those who did not applaud were noticed, and in time their political standing or careers suffered. At the store to which I referred, my wife did not applaud, and her lack of enthusiasm and occasional criticism of store policies were noticed, and she was eventually fired. She was too independent, as her husband could earn enough for his family, and her life did not depend on her job. The store preferred to hire ladies who were in some distress, divorced or with many children, who expressed the expected enthusiasm and did not question anything.

Under Communism, there were no economically independent people. All the businesses were "nationalized" and transferred to the ownership of the state. The last economically independent people were the farmers, until the introduction of collectivism, when they were transformed into wage workers. Everybody's means of subsistence were controlled by the state. Eventually people became poor and spent their time in long lines for food. Their preoccupation was to get something on their children's table and they had no time for political opposition. In a similar way but a somewhat different style, when in a free society people are drowning in debt, they have to swallow everything from their bosses and they have no time or means for political action. One has to quietly suffer many indignities.

My hope is that this book will inspire some of my readers to show courage. There is no need for revolution and violence, only for a quiet and subtle opposition, in which human dignity triumphs over fear.

**

This is my story, as I developed from a scared child to a young man, in the confrontation with a mighty totalitarian system. I was not a hero, nor had the material of a martyr, but at a certain point I decided that in my freedom as a human being I could make a stand. I was not eager for a fight, but I became a reluctant dissident. My fight was quiet and low profile.

I am a Transylvanian by birth, and now a Romanian American. Unlike what one may believe from the Hollywood movies, the people of Transylvania were not blood sucking vampires but gentle and kind. We were not cruel and did not oppress others, but we were the oppressed for the longest time of our history, at least until 1918 when Transylvania was united with Romania.

Romanians in general are not given to extremes. They are not swayed by metaphysical arguments and they do not believe the politicians who come with great promises. They doubt great and seductive political philosophies. They have little respect for rulers and rules, particularly when such rules contradict common sense.

The Communists took power in Romania at the end of the Second World War, on the strength of the Soviet armies occupying the country. There were less than 1,000 Party members at the end of the war, and they stood no chance to win elections. When such elections took place in the late 40s, the results were falsified. The leaders of the democratic parties, popular and respected, were arrested and thrown in prisons, where most of them died.

The initial power in the Party was held by Ana Pauker, a former Comintern leader coming from the Soviet Union. She realized that, as a Jewish woman, she may have a hard time controlling the country, so she promoted Gheorghe Gheorghiu Dej to the top while remaining the power behind the throne. In the 50s, Dej got rid of he, after obtaining approval from Moscow, where Stalin was becoming more and more anti-Semitic. Some of her associates were thrown in prison, where they died, but she was allowed to retire under house arrest.

Dej was such a submissive and conformist leader that Khrushchev decided to withdraw his troops from Romania after a visit in which Dej treated him like an emperor. After the withdrawal of the troops, Dej started to take a more independent line. The Soviets were disturbed by the Romanian duplicity, but now they could do little about it. Unfortunately, Dej died in 1964 (after secretly receiving the last rites from the patriarch of the Romanian Orthodox Church).

A fight for power broke out at the top of the Party, in good Communist tradition. Various fractions agreed on Nicolae Ceaușescu to be the new leader of the Party, as a stop-gap measure until a better man would be found. Once in power, Ceaușescu eliminated all his rivals, promoted his own men and took complete control of the Party. The population liked him when he condemned some of the abuses of the 50s, and then in 1968 expressed opposition to the Soviet invasion of Czechoslovakia, but the honeymoon did not last for too long. In the early 70s he became a tyrant, suppressing some modest freedoms that the citizens enjoyed.

At the time when I grew up, the Communist Party was in total control of the country. This extended from the economy, industry, and agriculture, to culture and education. Religion was considered a sad inheritance from the past to be slowly suppressed and eventually eliminated. Education was supposed to promote atheism, monasteries and churches were closed, and the number of priests and pastors reduced. There was still some toleration of religion, as long as it remained in the shadows, without any power to influence the new generation or society in general.

***

The stories in this book are entirely real and I aimed to be as truthful as possible. This should not be interpreted in an absolute sense. I did not remember the exact words of some dialogs, but they took place very much as described here. As forty years or more passed since this story took place, and my memory consists of sometimes unrelated fragments, I was not sure of some dates or the exact order of some events, but any possible mistake is unintentional. As for the stories about other people, I gathered them from my family, relatives and friends.

I will start with the story of my maternal grandfather and my father, who played a large role in my life, being at the same time interesting and representative characters for those times. My mother had an even higher influence on me, but that was deep and subtle, beyond some particular events.

The Stoic

A few weeks after the break of the First World War, Ilie Turlea – my maternal grandfather – was forced to join the Austria-Hungarian army. He was recently married. I have the picture of him and his beautiful young wife, Valeria, in which she sits and he stands next to her dressed in an Austrian soldier uniform. She looks calm and thoughtful, with a barely visible smile which could be interpreted either as innocence or as shrewdness. His face, with high cheek bones, is frozen and inscrutable. He is a man used to hard work - powerful, but at the same time resigned to the fate of a soldier sent to fight for a cause in which he does not believe. The picture was taken just as he was to embark for a long travel to Galicia, where the first major action of the war between Austria and Russia was about to take place.

The Romanians from Transylvania, sent to fight for Austria-Hungary, had no heart for it. A Romanian song from that time begged, "Emperor, emperor, sue for peace, do not fight." Romanians formed the unprivileged class in Transylvania and the Hungarian authorities were making great efforts to eliminate their language and culture. The Romanian elite – doctors, professors, lawyers – could speak Hungarian in addition to their own language, and they sent their children to study in Budapest, or more commonly, at a prestigious university in Vienna, at a time when the city was at the peak of its intellectual and artistic development. Most Romanian peasants were working on the large latifundia owned by Hungarian nobles, whom they called "grofi", perhaps a corruption of the German term "graf" – count.

18

It was not always like that. Hungarians arrived in Transylvania in the ninth century and by the eleven century they were the masters of the province. For a time, there were both Hungarian and Romanian nobles, such as John Hunyadi, the father of one of the greatest kings of Hungary, Matthias Corvinus. John was a major political figure in East Europe, a fighter against the Ottoman Turks, for which he was named Athleta Christi by the Pope.

As the centuries past, the Romanian nobles disappeared, perhaps most of them absorbed into the Hungarian nobility. The Romanians were left at the bottom of the social pyramid. An agreement was reached in the fifteen century, called Unio Trium Nationum – the Union of the Three Nations – in which the Hungarians, Germans and Székelys (a separate group, which was otherwise speaking Hungarian) declared cooperation, equality and brotherhood. The Romanians were not even mentioned.

Romanians started to gain consciousness as a separate people in a strange way. In the year 1700, they were tricked by two Jesuit priests to sign a union with Rome, in which they would keep their Orthodox faith and traditions but accept the authority of the Pope. In exchange, they would be recognized as an official nationality in the Hungarian kingdom, with the same privileges as the other nationalities. Many Orthodox priests and bishops agreed, although some refused, and among those some were killed. Tragically, the Romanians never received what was promised, as it was only a trick to bring them in line. There was, however, an unexpected side effect.

A group of bright young Romanians was sent to Rome, to get their theological education there, at the heart of the Catholic world. In Rome, they learned Italian for the day-to-day conversations, but also Latin, needed for their theological education. They were surprised to notice the similarities between these languages and the Romanian language. Studying history, they learned that the territory from which they were coming was once a Roman province, from 105 to 275 after Christ. Their conclusion was that the Romanians are descendants of the Romans and can claim a more noble origin than their masters, the Hungarians, who came from the Asian steppes much later. They returned to their country, where they became priests, bishops or teachers in the institutes of higher learning. From their positions, they spread this awareness of noble origin and started a movement to grant Romanians their rightful position in society.

In 1848, Hungarians revolted against the Austrian domination, and under their leader Lajos Kossuth, took arms to gain their independence. All nationalities should be equal! That was an attractive call for all oppressed people, and Romanians responded, asking that in a new independent Hungary, Romanians should be given equal rights with the Hungarians. Kossuth was shocked and answered with a definite No. Equality is for the noble people, the Hungarians, not for the lowly Romanians. Romanians and Hungarians ended fighting each other, giving Austria the opportunity to defeat both.

By 1914, the Romanians' struggle for equality did not lead to any significant improvement of their lot. They were still at the bottom of the society and their language was suppressed.

***

Now Ilie was asked to go fight and maybe die for the power and the glory of Austria- Hungary, which was at the same time was oppressing his people. He was not a nationalist or a revolutionary, and as a humble man, he took the Austrian uniform and went to war.

He joined other Romanian recruits and they were shipped to fight in the Galicia campaign, in what is now southern Poland. The Austrians were initially winning, but soon were overwhelmed and started to lose battles. Ilie saw some of his childhood friends die. He told us how once, while in the trenches, one of his fellow soldiers was curious to stand up and look around. When against his friend's advice he raised his head to peak, he was instantly shot dead by a sniper. They were eventually surrounded, most were killed, but Ilie survived and was taken prisoner by the Russians.

As expected, the prisoners were shipped back to Russia. They travelled by train, from camp to camp, perhaps for weeks and months. They were treated well – this was quite different from the Second World War when Russians and Germans hated each other and killed their prisoners by starvation or overwork. After a while, the Russian government thought that the prisoners may be dangerous and a burden for a Russia about to collapse, and a decision was made to send them east. They traveled by train again, crossing the Ural Mountains into Siberia and moved further and further East, until they reached some place close to the border with China.

***

21

This unfortunate group of prisoners where Ilie belonged arrived at their Siberian destination in the middle of the winter, when the temperature was below what they had ever experienced. They were disembarked from the train and marched on foot towards a remote village, the place where they were supposed to remain. Now their Russian guards did not have to prevent an escape. If one ran away, he would die frozen in the Siberian barren wilderness. They walked for hours, with little breaks to rest. The group had a carriage pulled by horses, from where some food was occasionally dispensed. If a prisoner developed frostbite, he was allowed to hop into the carriage and take care of his feet or hands.

After hours of marching, Ilie felt totally exhausted. In the beginning he was thinking of his village, of his beautiful wife, of children running through the vineyards on a sunny September day, of girls singing at the harvest, of grapes filled with sweetness and perfume. All those images started to slowly fade, replaced by one thought: I must survive this. The mind said go, but the body could no longer do it. Still, he did not give up on life and tried to find a way to survive. He remembered that the prisoners with frostbite were allowed into the carriage. During a short break, he pulled off his boots and filled them with snow and ice. He was sure that his toes would freeze, and then he would be allowed in a carriage and he would survive.

After another hour of excruciating pain and total exhaustion, there was another break and he sat down to examine his feet. He took off his boots. The snow and ice inside had melted into a hot liquid, with vapors coming out of it. The strong life inside him defeated death. He knew he would not only live but would also return home not as a

22

handicapped casualty of war, but a healthy man able to work in the fields.

The village where they stayed was not guarded. There was no way for a prisoner to travel back to home from this remote Siberian village. He was placed in a home where he lived as any ordinary Russian peasant. When the spring and summer came, he joined the people of the village for their work in the fields. He could have sabotaged them, slowing down and helping them as little as possible, but he did the opposite. To not work would have been a denial of his youth, of his vigor and of his self-worth as a strong, intelligent and reliable man. He learned to speak Russian and lived a normal life, as if he had always been there.

A year passed, then another, then another. The Russian revolution took place in November of 1917, and the war ended in November of 1918. Both events were hardly registered in the remote Siberian village. The people there cared little about politics, revolutions and European wars. In 1919, although not a prisoner any more, he was not yet allowed to leave and return to his country. The prisoners in Siberia seemed forgotten by the world until 1920, when the famous Norwegian explorer Fridtjof Nansen started an initiative to find and repatriate lost and forgotten prisoners of war.

The people in the village tried to convince him to forget his family and country and remain there. They told him, "We like you very much. We have beautiful and hard-working girls here. You can marry one of them, have children and live all your life with us." That was attractive for many reasons, but he told them why he wanted to go back: he had left a wife and old parents behind.

I do not know how long his trip back lasted, perhaps weeks or months. He arrived in another country than the one he left. The Austria-Hungarian empire, in which various "secondary" nationalities had 10 million more people than the "primary" (Austrians and Hungarians), did not exist anymore. New countries, such as Czechoslovakia and Yugoslavia were formed. In December of 1918, Transylvania joined Romania, to the great joy of the millions of Romanians who formed the majority in the province. For the second time in history, Romanians belonged to a single country. The Union was declared in Alba Iulia, my home town, which was barely six miles away from Șard, the village of my grandfather. (The first union had happened under Michael the Brave, in 1600.)

Ilie arrived in his village unannounced. Perhaps most people, including his wife, thought he was long dead, as they did not hear from him after 1914. I wish I could see the scene in which he and his wife met after six years of separation and silence.

The following years were some of the best in his life. In 1921, the Romanian parliament passed an agrarian reform law. All properties with more than about 250 acres were broken in smaller lots, which were distributed to the peasants who were working on them. The old *grofi* who did not take Romanian citizenship but went to Hungary lost their entire land.

No longer part of an oppressed minority, free, with all the land that he can work, Ilie lunched himself into hard work to manage and grow his farm. He – as other families in his village – had multiple lots. Some were cultivated with corn, some with wheat, some with legumes, but the most important were the vineyards. He favored the best varieties of grapes, one of them the Muscat Ottonel, which produced a perfumed wine, but without the usual sweetness of other the Muscat varieties. His vineyards produced more and more, and he sold wine, insuring a significant income from his family.

In the spring and summer, he woke at four o'clock in the morning and was in the filed shortly after five. He worked all day and went to sleep around nine, when it started to get dark. Managing multiple lots with a variety of cultures required not only hard work, but also a lot of smart management, as various tasks had to be executed on precise days. A delay in planting or harvesting might have compromised the production of a particular lot. He also multiplied the animals of his farm, increasing the number of sheep, cows, chicken and pigs. The farm was entirely self-sustained, and, as we would say today, ecological. He did not use fertilizers, but the manure from the cows, which were fed from what the land produced.

One of the initiatives he took required a hard work. He purchased additional land on the sunny hills around the village, land which was never cultivated before. He cleaned the weeds and the shrubs, removed the stones and prepared the soil to plant grapes. This was back breaking work and a less vigorous and determined man could not have done it. It was not only hard, but with no immediate rewards, as the vine took a number of years to grow and give good grapes.

Eventually his farm grew, and he was producing so much that at harvest time he had to employ workers to help. Most of the farm hired hands were coming from the Western Carpathian Mountains, where the intensive agriculture could not be practiced, and the people were poorer. He treated them well, paid them in time and generously.

He participated in the councils of his village and was respected by all people. On a number of occasions, he lent money to other farmers in need, and on more than one occasion, when they could not pay him back, forgave their debts.

His wife Valeria gave him a son, Aurel, who died shortly after his birth. In 1925 she gave him a daughter, Aurelia, who was to become my mother. Unfortunately, Valeria died young, in 1930, of pneumonia. Later he married another woman, also called Valeria.

The prosperous times did not last forever. In 1941, Romania entered the Second World War on the side of Germany. The initial objective was to recover Basarabia, a province occupied by the Soviet Union after the Molotov Ribbentrop pact, but after this was achieved, hundreds of thousands of Romanian soldiers were killed trying to take Crimea and then at Stalingrad. When the tide of war changed, and the Soviet armies were at our borders, Romania switched sides, denounced the alliance with Germany and joined the Allies. At the same time, the Soviet armies came over Romania and soon a Communist government took power in the country. The tragedy of the Communist rule was just starting.

Ilie did not care for politics. His world consisted of his family, of his church and of his farm. Unfortunately, the Communist regime cared about people like him. He belonged to the social class of rich peasants, called *chiaburi* by the Communist propaganda. They were considered dangerous, as they could not be controlled or manipulated. The workers in the factories and the bureaucrats depended on the regime for their jobs and salaries. The intellectuals could be marginalized and forced to submit to the Communist ideology to be allowed to publish. However, the rich peasants did not care. They were entirely self-sustained and did not need to shout the Communist slogans in order to harvest the vineyards or to feed their animals. Insomuch as they were independent, they were dangerous.

The regime started to systematically destroy the chiaburi. The first move was to impose quotas in the form of products to be delivered to the state. They were fixed in such a way to ruin the rich peasants.

One may think that the Communist Government was playing Robin Hood, taking from the rich to give to the poor, but that was not the case. First, they gave nothing to the poor. The so-called rich peasants were the men who fought in the trenches of the First World War and then lost their sons at Stalingrad in the Second World War. Others were people who emigrated to the United States before the First World War, worked hard in the mines of Ohio and Pennsylvania, then returned after the war and purchased land and established prosperous farms. All these people were not rich by inheritance or by manipulation, but through hard work. They were not even rich by today's standards, but only middle class. They were the most productive people in the Romanian economy and they produced so much as to make the country a great exporter of agricultural products. These were the people who had to be destroyed.

My mother told me of a scene she saw, which broke her heart. She was with my grandfather Ilie helping him in the field. An assessor came to talk with him, and he said he had to submit so much of his harvest to the state. It was not a percentage, but an absolute figure, which otherwise amounted to perhaps 90% of what his farm produced. Ilie was stunned and asked to discuss this more and come to some more reasonable figure. At that point, the assessor turned and walked away. Ilie ran after him to continue the conversation, but the man refused to talk anymore. Ilie knew he was doomed.

After many peasant farms were bankrupt, the state made the second move: collectivization. The idea was to join all the private land into collective farms, where the peasants would work together. All the operations and the products of the collective were to be controlled by the state. In this way, the peasants were transformed from proud owners and entrepreneurs into daily wage workers, without rights and without any independent initiatives.

Commissions were set to manage the collectivization process. A commission would come to a village and call the farm owners one by one, asking them to sign their land to the collective farm. First, they were told of the benefits (nobody believed in them), then they were threatened. The ones who resisted were passed to the Securitate, who arrested them. They were accused of anti-state activities and sentenced to many years of hard labor. Some were outright killed, some others disappeared in the labor camps.

My mother told me that one late evening she heard somebody knocking at our door, and to her surprise, it was my grandfather. He asked to sleep at our house, as he was trying to evade the collectivization commission, which was coming to his village the next day. He stayed a few days with us, but it was hopeless. Eventually he returned and signed, so little was left from the hard work of more than thirty years. They were only allowed to keep some small lots around the house, to feed their own families.

The former prosperous peasants, who by now were nothing but poor wage workers, had no interest in their work. They showed up in the fields to be directed by the farm managers, but often they only made believe they worked. The farms were now led by loyal Communist Party people, some of them from the same village. These were people who were previously less prosperous, not because of fate, but because they were less capable to manage their land or drank too much or neglected their work. Such people were often envious of the more prosperous ones and now it was time to take revenge.

The agricultural production started to take a nose dive. Everybody knew it, but the newspapers reported about the enthusiasm of the peasants, about their happy brotherhood in the newly created collective farms and about the amazing increase in the output from the land.

Some years after the collectivization process was finished, my mother came home with tears in her eyes. She told me she walked next to a fenced land holding cows. The cows were only skeletons – they looked sick and dirty. She even saw one fall down and not rise again. My mother felt pity for them and told me how on my grandfather's farm the cows were well taken care of, how they were fat, strong, clean and well-groomed.

***

I spent many days at my grandfather's house. Sometimes my mother would take me there and leave me with my relatives for several days, sometimes for a whole week. I was a city boy and greatly enjoyed playing with children my age in the countryside. Every Sunday morning, he shaved, put on his best clothes, and went to attend liturgy at the village Orthodox church. My Baptist mother did not allow me to go with him, although I wanted to.

One summer day, when I was about ten years old, my grandfather took me with him to a field about five miles away from his house. We loaded the hay into a large cart pulled by oxen to bring home and store in a shed next to the house. We worked together for about an hour, loaded the cart and started on our way home. As we moved slowly on the road, the sky became covered with dark clouds, and a heavy and violent summer rain started. I wanted to walk next to him, but he placed me in the cart on top of the hay and covered me with some clothes. From under the clothes, I could still see him walking next to the oxen.

He was calm and sure of himself. He must have been seventy at that time, but he had a strong body that showed no sign of age, disease or exhaustion. He was hit by the rain and the wind, completely soaked, and the powerful muscles were visible from under his shirt. He walked without any rush, totally oblivious to the rain and the deafening thunders. He carried in him the trenches of the First World War, the Siberian cold winters and the hard work of the field. My spirit was touched, but I could not know why at that time and at that age. Now I can see it better.

From what little I remember about him, I never detected the smallest scintilla of bitterness or self-pity. I rarely saw him laugh or waste his time in trivial pursuits.

He transcended the frivolous pleasures as he transcended the vagrancies of life. In his last years, he continued to work on his much smaller lots, took care of the animals, and without fail attended the services of the Orthodox church. The walls of his house were adorned with icons of Christ, of martyrs and of archangels, and inside the prayers were said at the appointed times.

***

In 1973, Ilie was diagnosed with prostate cancer. He refused treatment and wanted to die at home, with his family and his farm and his animals. He did not cling to life, as his mission was finished and there was no point in extending it for few extra weeks or months in some dirty hospital room.

We received the news of his passing on a day in December, and my mother cried. I barely remember his funeral, only that it was very cold. He was laid next to his first wife, Valeria, in the cemetery which surrounds the village church.

The tomb holding his bones is just a few yards away from the entrance to the church, from the icons of Christ and the martyrs and the archangels. But these are only bones and images. The real Ilie is now with the real Christ and with the real angels.

AN ACCIDENTAL DISSIDENT

The Adapter

On the left bank of the Mureș River (known as Maris by the Romans), which crosses Transylvania and leaves Romania to join the Tisa river in Hungary, there is a village called Straja. It is situated about six miles from Alba Iulia, the city which was once the capital of Transylvania. Straja stands on the north slope of a small mountain and it does not get too much sunlight. Because of its position, the people here were generally poorer than those of the other villages around Alba Iulia, for instance, my mother's village, Șard, which was facing south and had its land enriched by the occasional floods of the Ampoi River. They needed additional wit and perseverance to overcome their disadvantages.

In this village lived the Oara family, consisting of the husband Nicolae, the wife Antinia, and their four children. The oldest was a daughter, Ana, and she was followed by three brothers: Mihai, Ioan and Vasile. Together, they covered some of the most common names in Romania at that time. Mihai was my father. For some reason, the people in those parts did not like fancy names, so I was also called Mihai. My grandmother insisted that I should also be called Ioan, in memory of my uncle who died in Czechoslovakia in the Second World War. In Șard, my mother's village, people used fancy Roman names. Among my many uncles and aunts and cousins, I have names of emperors and Roman ladies: Aurelian, Aurelia, Traian, Decebal (a Dacian king), Valer, Valeria, Sanflora, Lucrecia, Letizia.

Both Mihai and Ioan were soldiers during the Second World War - my father from the beginning of the war, my uncle towards the end. Yet my father survived the war and my uncle was killed.

I know that in war one soldier may live and another may die. This happens at random, and the human mind is always in a state of wonder as to why it is so. The one who survives asks himself why he lives while his friend is dead. However, for the two brothers, Mihai and Ioan, it was not the random bullet that decided their fate. They made choices which lead to their destinies. They faced moral dilemmas, and each came with a different solution.

At the age of fourteen, my father had to leave his village and come to the city of Alba Iulia to look for employment. This was the way of boys from poor families. They had to take care of themselves at the earliest age possible to ease the family from some of their financial burdens.

He was short, with a round and almost cherubic face, radiating a certain degree of easiness, friendship and sweetness, but behind this façade of bonhomie, he had a sharp mind and a shrewd character. He knew where to find the things his master wanted, how to resolve minor conflicts, how to get things his way and always fall on his feet. His first job was as a busboy at a bowling alley owned by a Jewish man.

He started his military service, mandatory at that time, just before the start of the Second World War. His commanders found him technologically smart and reliable, and assigned him to a communication battalion attached to the 20th Infantry Division, where he was trained in telephony.

When the war started, the Romanian armies first crossed the Prut river, which separated half of the Romanian province of Moldova from the other half, taken by the Soviet Union through the Molotov-Ribbentrop Pact. That was the logic behind the alliance with Germany: to take back the Romanian territories snatched by the Soviet Union. After Bessarabia and Northern Bukovina were recovered, the big question was if Romania should continue its participation in the war. Most Romanian generals and politicians were of the option that the armies should stop there, but the Romanian leader, General Ion Antonescu, decided to continue. This was not done out of loyalty for Hitler, but because it would have placed Romania in a better position after the war and helped to get an ascendancy over the old enemy, Hungary, which had also snatched some Romanian territories in northern Transylvania.

Calculations like these mean nothing for common soldiers. They are too complicated and remote from their lives. Why would a Romanian soldier fight in Russia in 1942? To recover Bessarabia? That had already happened. To win glory in battles? That was not in the Romanian ethos and character. To fight Communism? Who cared about Communism? The Romanian soldier did not fight for any of these reasons. He fought only because he had to, because he was ordered and there was no way out.

After taking Bessarabia, the 3rd and 4th Romanian armies went to fight at Odessa, in Crimea and in Caucasus, with heavy losses. In the summer of 1942, they were sent to defend the flanks of the German Army which were fighting to conquer Stalingrad. The Romanians were just auxiliaries in relation to the Germans, relegated to lower and less strategic tasks. When they noticed extensive preparation on the Soviet side for a counterattack and encirclement, they notified the Germans, who did not take them seriously. Romanians asked for anti-tank equipment, but the Germans provided none. All their cries of alarm were interpreted as the whining of cowards.

We know now that the Russians attacked and encircled and destroyed the German armies at Stalingrad. It was the first major strategic defeat suffered by Hitler. The Russians executed a two-pronged attack: one in the north, where the Romanian 3rd Army was placed, and one in the south, guarded by the Romanian 4rd Army. The 4th Army resisted for a couple of days. They were ordered to fight to the last man, which they did. To what purpose? In the south, the Romanian 3rd Army was annihilated in a matter of hours. Among them was the 91st Regiment of the 20th Division Infantry, to which my father belonged. But he was not there.

Sometime in 1941 or in 1942, my father had a secret discussion with another soldier, who advised him how to avoid the front. The lower grade soldiers have their own world, in which they learn how to orient themselves, gain advantages here and there, and avoid trouble. It is a secret world, perhaps impenetrable to the higher ranks. These were not voluntary soldiers, but young people taken from their families and farm, where they would tend sheep, harvest corn and gather grapes to make good wine. Their main goal in the military was not to win but to survive. My father's friend taught him how to survive by faking an eye illness.

The secret consisted of some concoction to be applied to the eyes. It was a secret formula, just like the Greek Fire or medieval poisons. When applied, the eyelids start to swell, and the eyes become itchy, red, and swollen, shedding rivers of tears. It looked like a serious eye infection. The nice thing was, that while it seemed serious, the symptoms would completely disappear after a few weeks, leaving no permanent damage.

My father used this concoction a few days before his regiment, the 91st Infantry of the 20th Division, was set to embark on trains and go deep into Russia. He was promptly sent to a military hospital, somewhere in the south of Romania. To his surprise, the hospital was filled with young soldiers having similar symptoms. It looked like the secret was not restrained to a small circle, but the formula was used by dozens or even hundreds of soldiers. Moreover, the doctors were not stupid and could easily figure out that this was a self-inflicted condition. The rest of the regiment went to Russia and most were killed, beautiful young lads who were supposed to inherit the farms and produce food for the whole country and take care of their parents in their old age. Fewer than 5% of the Romanian soldiers at Stalingrad returned alive.

In all armies of the world, self-mutilation with the purpose of avoiding fighting is a serious offense, in most cases punished by death. I suppose the laws were the same in Romania. There was, however, something in the Romanian character which did not fit this law. When choosing between big words, big ideologies, and common sense, Romanians prefer the latter. I saw this in many cases. In my youth, I saw people listening for hours to some propaganda activist who spoke about the great future and happiness expected for us under Communism. People applauded, but nobody believed. I read accounts of Jewish people in Odessa, hidden in some houses, who were able to bribe the Romanian police and were left alone. They could not bribe the Germans. More recently, when NATO bombed Serbia, Romania pledged support and forbade the export of oil to that country, but hundreds of small trucks loaded with gasoline were crossing the border to Serbia. It must have been the same with the military doctors. They had their orders to catch the soldiers with self-induced diseases. The official position was that Romania had to make a great sacrifice to defeat the old enemy, the Communist Soviet Union, and ensure a place in the world together with her ally, Nazi Germany. But here were these young men, and their mothers who were praying every night for their sons in front of the Virgin Mary's icons. The doctors had to choose who they were going to help: the great Axis powers or the farmer boys. They chose the latter.

My father stayed a few weeks in the hospital and came home completely cured. By that time, his regiment was deep into Russia and he was assigned to another unit, which stayed behind in the city of Alba Iulia. His friends and superiors died in the frozen fields of Russia from the cold, or blown up by tanks, or sprayed with bullets. The few who survived the initial assault and were taken prisoner, died later of wounds, cold, and famine. My father survived, and so now I can write this story.

In the summer of 1944, a great danger was facing the country. The tide of the war had changed: the German armies were being defeated everywhere, and now the Russian armies were at the border. Antonescu, the Romanian general, who tied the destiny of Romania to Germany, was desperately trying to get in touch with the

Allies, the United States and England, to sue for peace. His diplomatic overtures were rejected, as they asked Romania to first come to an agreement with the USSR, Romania's archenemy. Peace with the Soviet Union was much harder to achieve. Romania wanted protection but could not get it.

Antonescu vacillated and eventually decided to continue the war on the side of Germany. This meant that the territory of Romania was to become a war zone, with all the harm and destruction which was to follow. A conspiracy was organized between King Michael and some of the important political parties. On August 23rd, 1944, a group of officers designated by the conspirators arrested Antonescu when he came to an audience with the King. Romania changed sides. The Germans troops were disarmed, and Romania pledged allegiance to the anti-Nazi powers. The Soviet troops entered the country. Theoretically they were allies, but they behaved more like occupiers.

Romania had to bring its own contribution to the war against Germany. Surprisingly, Romania had the fourth-largest army fighting the Nazis, after the Soviet Union, the United States, and England. (France was out of action for most of the war.) Romanian troops continued the fight into Hungary and Czechoslovakia. Many Romanian soldiers had to die so the country would have a voice when peace was discussed. In reality, the destiny of the country was already decided when Churchill wrote on a napkin the post-war formula for Romania and Greece. The Soviets would have 90% influence in Romania and England 90% influence in Greece.

My father's brother, Ioan, was called to join the military in 1944 and soon after that he was supposed to be shipped to fight in Czechoslovakia. My father tried to save him, advising him how to use the same formula for a false eye disease. Apparently, my uncle Ion was a much more scrupulous person than my father. He was also shy and less daring. He refused and went to the front.

Sometime in the winter of 1945, my father received a telegram telling him that his brother was wounded – his leg was blown to pieces – and he was in a military hospital in Bucharest. My father was given permission to leave his unit and took a fast train to Bucharest, then went straight to the hospital, where he found his brother dead. The only thing my father was able to do was to participate in a military funeral and mark his tomb so that he and his parents could visit it later. I suppose that my father visited the tomb at least a few times in the following years, when he had business in Bucharest. By now, nobody knows where that tomb is. Few people even remember that there was once a young man called Ion who died in Czechoslovakia in the winter of 1944. I believe I am the last to remember him in my prayers.

* * *

The war was over, and my father was released from the Army. As he was already trained in telephony, he got a job as a technician, maintaining telephone exchanges in the city. When the Communist Party came to power, they needed to increase its membership, so they recruited a large number of members. My father fit the profile, having what was called a 'healthy origin," being from a poor family. He was poorly educated but possessed a natural intelligence, he was sociable and even popular. Then something unexpected happened: he was appointed the President of the Popular Council of the city of Alba Iulia, a job equivalent with that of a mayor – in fact, the people in the city called him mayor. Even now I find it hard to believe that my father was at one point the mayor of the city that was once the capital of Transylvania - the city of king and princes, of bishops and local assemblies of nobles. Unfortunately, at that time the city had lost its importance, as its prestige was undermined by the Communist Party, which saw it as a nest of nationalistic pride. The legends and the heroes of the past had to be forgotten and replaced with the new ones, such as the illegal Communist who fought the fascists and the worker who produced more than the plan required.

My father was a good mayor. Older people told me that he was highly respected and during his time, the city was clean, the garbage was collected, and the citizens were treated with respect. He was not the typical Communist local leader - harsh, arrogant and autocratic. He treated everybody with honor and solved the citizens' problems in a friendly manner. He could have had a great future, ending in some important position in Bucharest, with a villa on the elite Primaverii quarter of the city. But, on the other hand, he could not go so far, as he was too humane for that.

His bosses at the district level called him one day with a request: paint all yard fences in the city white. This request had some hidden political agenda. Fences in the countryside were painted white for precise reasons: to prevent the spread of parasitic insects, which could not survive on white paint. In time, villages were recognized as villages by the white paint on the fences, and cities were recognized by the fact that they did not have white fences. By painting the fences of Alba Iulia white, the Communist Party was degrading the city to the level of a village. There were cities which were slated for development and growth, especially those with many factories and a high concentration of workers. Alba Iulia was not in that category. Its pride were the cathedrals, museums, and the large medieval citadel.

My father objected. He tried many stratagems to avoid fulfilling the order. He brought many arguments and delayed as much as he could, but to no avail. Eventually, he was given a deadline by which he had to complete the task.

Just a few days before the deadline, he decided to take a dramatic step. He took the night train to Bucharest and asked for an emergency audience with the Minister of Internal Affairs, Ioan Dreghici. I do not know what he told the minister. Maybe he appealed to his patriotism or he told him that citizens of the city would become antagonistic to the Party. Somehow, he succeeded, and he came back home the next day with a paper in his hand by which the minister was rescinding the order of the local district. The city was saved, but after a few days my father was dismissed. I'm sure he did not take it hard, as he had no political ambitions. For a while, he was some kind of city inspector, but then reverted to his humble job of a telephony technician.

At the time when he was mayor, he married a girl from a nearby village. They purchased some land in the city and he build a small house, which was later enlarged. His wife died after five years and left him a widow with a four-year-old daughter. That was the time when he met my mother.

When I grew up, he was a member of the Communist Party but also a devoted Orthodox Christian, attending church regularly. For me, these two were incompatible, but not for him. He told the Communists what they wanted to hear but kept the faith of his ancestors. He was officially a Communist, but secretly he despised them, which made it very easy for him to lie about his belief in Communist ideology. He remained a Christian, loved his Church and believed in her teachings.

The Coward

In a way, I owe my life to wine. Some time after he became a widower, my father went on an expedition to the Ampoi Valley in search of good wine. In Șard, people told him to look for Ilie Turlea, who had excellent wine for sale. He went to his house, they talked, and Ilie gave him wine from different years to taste. One of the best varieties was Muscat Ottonel, which had the taste of Muscat, without being too sweet. It was very good, he would buy some. He also noticed Ilie's daughter, Aurelia, and found that she was not married. She was divorced at that time. She left and divorced her previous husband, who lived in a village far from Alba Iulia, because he was an incorrigible womanizer.

My father continued to come and buy wine, and eventually invited my mother to meet him in the city of Alba Iulia where he lived. When he showed enough interest in her, my mother was wise enough to ask some of her acquaintances from Alba Iulia about my father. Everybody, without exception, gave her the best references possible. Yes, he was a good man, moral, hardworking, and kind. She looked with suspicion at the unanimity of opinion and thought it must be some conspiracy.

They married in the spring of 1954, and I was born exactly nine months after. It was a small miracle, as my mother could not have children before or after me.

We were rich and poor at the same time. We could not afford a phone, a radio, a car or a TV set, but we had a

44

house with a yard in which we grew chicken and sometimes a pig. We heated the house by burning wood in stoves. My father went every autumn to the mountains to purchase wood to be used during the winter. The logs had to be cut in smaller parts and stowed, and I became skilled in splitting logs and starting a fire. Unlike many modern families today, we had no mortgage to pay as my parents built the house step by step with their own hands and with the help of family and friends. I knew nothing about consumer debt, even graduating college with zero debt. We had a stable and loving family, in which the parents lived moral lives and invested in the education of their children.

I consider myself blessed to have been born and to have grown in the Transylvanian city of Alba Iulia, filled with history and culture and tradition, and to have played with my friends on the bastions of a large medieval citadel.

By the time I was born, my mother was already considering leaving the Orthodox Church to join the Baptists. I do not know all the details which would explain this conversion, but I think it might have been related to the troubles she had in her first marriage and the emotional support she was able to receive from some of her Baptist acquaintances. One of the immediate consequences for me was that, while (as a concession to my father) she agreed to my baptism as a baby in the Orthodox Church, she later took me to the local Baptist church. She was the dominant figure in the family, so she decided the religion of her children – both myself and my sister Maria. In perspective, our family took a strange religious journey: she was born and grew up Orthodox, but later she became Baptist. I grew up as a Baptist, but later in life I returned to the Orthodox Church, completing a full circle of our faith.

Belief in Jesus was serene and comforting for the first years of my life, but became troubled later by the time I was twelve or thirteen. My sister was six years older than me and I started to browse and then read her school manuals. This is how I found out about evolution, which explained the origin and development of life on earth differently than the story I knew from the Bible. As I was already interested in science, this completely fascinated me. It was not only the theory of evolution itself, but a whole view of life and the universe which was rational, logical, scientific, and did not need a God to explain anything. I read and read from my sister's manuals and from books borrowed from the local library. While a new philosophy started to develop in my mind, I did not speak about it with anybody, but kept my thoughts secret, as I knew that these new concepts would come in contradiction with my mother's beliefs and I was afraid of her. I kept mulling and musing about science and faith, and at a certain point – I do not remember exactly when – I crossed the threshold and decided that I did not believe in God, I was an atheist. I was, however, a closet atheist in a country with a Communist/Atheistic ideology. However, the Communist Party was far away, while my mother was close.

To find more books, I went to the city library, where I spent hours reading and browsing. After books on evolution, I started to read books about Marxism, which I found in abundance. For the first time, I encountered a philosophy which seemed to explain everything. I was especially interested in Marx and Engels' view of Christianity. I read some of Engels' writings, in which he presents Christianity as the winner of a contest of many sects and beliefs in antiquity. It was another kind of evolution, with patterns of mutations, survival of the fittest, and natural selection. Far from being a result of revelation, Christianity was simply the winner of this struggle. It provided consolation to the masses of slaves and poor people, and eventually the exploiting classes found it useful, as it kept the exploited numbed, content with their state in society. Religion was the opium for the masses, which had to be administered to prevent revolution. In Communism, where exploitation was to be abolished and the people to be free, religion would no longer play any role, and, as a superstition rejected by reason and science, it would wither away. The family, an expression of patriarchal domination, would also go away and be replaced by free love between free people. Fascinating!

There was, however, a dichotomy which I found hard to resolve. From my parents (and not only from them), I became aware of many evils perpetrated under the Communist regime. Why did the Communist Party take away the farms, including my grandfather's? Why was life in capitalist countries better than in socialist countries? Why did the Communist Party switch positions many times if they owned the scientific view of society? Why did Stalin institute terror in Russia? There was a natural, semi-official answer: those people did not know how to apply the correct doctrine of Communism. Besides that, I also knew that many of our leaders were nothing other than gangsters who took power for their own benefit.

At about the same time, I made another discovery, which became more important to me. One day, when I was in the fifth grade, at the age of eleven, I borrowed a book from the local library called *From the Multiplication Table to Integral*. I knew what the multiplication table was, but not the integral, and, because it looked mysterious and esoteric, I decided to figure it out. The book went through elementary algebra, which I found easy, then moved to more advanced algebra and finally to calculus.

I read a good explanation of the concept of a derivative and it made perfect sense to me. It was so clear and easy. I picked my sister's manuals from the tenth and eleventh grades and started to solve some of the math exercises. I was so satisfied finding that I can calculate the derivative of some functions. It was like the joy of driving for the first time. Yes, I could do it. I computed some easy derivatives, and then I learned tricks for how to solve the more difficult ones. Later, I graduated to the next level: integrals. I understood the deep mathematical significance (helping to compute areas under a function graph) and I was able to figure out the integral of various functions.

At the end of the fifth grade, I decided to take the challenge of solving problems from the *Mathematical Gazette*, a publication popular all over the country which attempted to stimulate and encourage middle and high school students who liked mathematics. During that summer vacation, I decided to attempt to solve a problem each day until I reached the critical number of ten, which was the minimum required to have one's name in the list of successful problem solvers. Between fun and games with my friends, I reserved some time for this, and soon I had fifteen problems solved. I carefully wrote the solutions, each one on a different sheet of paper, then I folded them, put them in an envelope and sent them to the *Mathematical Gazette* address in Bucharest.

I waited with anticipation for the arrival of the new edition of the *Gazette* in September. When it arrived, I quickly went to the last pages, where the successful solvers were listed by grade and alphabet. Yes, my name was there, with a (15) next to it, indicating the number of problems solved. I was in seventh heaven, happy as I could be. One morning, after school began, I came face-to-face with our school principal. He stopped me and shook my hand.

"Congratulations, Oara," he said, "you are the first student in the history of our school who has his name published as a problem solver in the *Mathematical Gazette*. You will be a great success. Keep doing it."

I realized that there was something different about me, both good and bad. Yes, I was a prodigy, doing high school calculus, but my life was burdened with a double secret: I was hiding to my mom that I was an atheist and I was hiding from my school that I was a Baptist. Day after day, I was terrified that either my mom or my school would discover who I really was. I looked with some envy at my friends, who seemed to be made of one piece while I was broken into many pieces. I found consolation in mathematics, which was pure, logical, rational, unemotional. It was not involved with politics, it did not condemn, and it did not cry.

***

Later, when I was still in the sixth grade, at the beginning of a class, the teacher told me that I must go to the principal's office. In the room, there was a group of students of various ages, and at first I could not make out what was common to all of us or why we were called. Then I realized: they were all children from Baptist families, whom I knew from our church, where my mother was taking me every Sunday. Some of them were even good friends.

In retrospect, I understood what was happening. The Communist authorities required that all schools execute certain activities related to atheistic education and – as much as possible – convince children not to attend church, especially the so-called "sects," of which the Baptists were one. The local schools were supposed to identify which children came from families involved with the sects and put pressure on them to abandon their faith. The local people may or may not have been convinced this was a good tactic, but they had to execute and report that it was done. That's why we were called. I do not believe our principal was passionate about atheism, but he had to go through all the moves.

So he did. While we stared at him like some stupid lambs taken to the butcher, he gave us some speech about the glorious future of our country, about the new peaks we would soon reach in the Communist era, and about science versus superstition. We had a duty to abandon all superstitions of the past and fully adopt the illuminated scientific worldview of the Communist Party. Then he became more specific, asking us to stop attending church. He ended by asking if we were ready to change our ways.

This was unfair and cruel. As children, we were under a double authority: that of the family and that of the school. We did not have the maturity and independence to make our own decisions and start fighting one authority or another. All the children were quiet. It was an awkward moment. This was even more unfair to me, as I was scolded for being a believer while in fact I was not, but that was hard to say.

At that time in my life, I was hungry for success and recognition. I was the child whom everybody praised, and I enjoyed it. I even considered myself superior to all the other students gathered in the principal's office. Finally, under the pressure of the moment, I stepped forward and said, "Comrade Principal, I do not really believe in God, but I go to church because my mother takes me there." I felt totally humiliated. The other children were quiet and looked at me perhaps as Jesus looked at Peter when he denied Him. The principal praised me and offered me as an example to the others. He could report to his superiors that the task was accomplished, one more off his checklist. We were dismissed and went back to our classes.

I felt like Judas after he betrayed Jesus. I was denying my parents, whom I loved; I treated them with disrespect. It did not matter that I was telling the truth, all that mattered was that I was a coward, paralyzed with fear, while the other Baptist children were courageous and did not betray. A few days later, I was walking next to a group of Baptist children, when one of them pointed at me and said, "He was scared and abandoned his faith." I made believe I did not hear. I did not tell anybody in my family about what happened, and I did not discuss it with any of my friends.

I hated Communism. I hated the school. I hated church and religion. I loved and hated my mother at the same time. I just wanted to be left alone. I was made into a coward, and for the next fifteen years of my life I struggled to redeem myself.

Not long after this episode, one evening while we were inside our house, my sister started to tell us about a funny situation she had witnessed the previous evening. She saw our school principal, a short and fat man around sixty years old, walking drunk in the street, occasionally leaning on the walls. It was funny, but it was also pathetic, as the principal of a local school should have been a straight and decent man, not one to make a fool of himself. I smiled with the rest of my family, and realized that people in positions of high authority were only human, with all the usual human mistakes and weaknesses. That was a good reason to fear them less than before.

In the eighth grade, before graduation, we were called to a meeting in which teachers and guests talked to us about our choices for the next phase of our lives. As most families wanted their children to attend high school, we were encouraged to also think about other paths. One could go to a professional school and become a valuable skilled worker, which would bring him or her a lot of satisfaction and success in life. We had only one factory in our city, which produced bricks for metallurgical furnaces. The factory was polluting and it was common knowledge that many people working there developed the disease of silicosis, which could be fatal. A worker from the factory came to talk with us and entice us to go and learn the skills and work there. Yes, there was a false rumor that some developed silicosis, but he, who worked there for many years, was the living proof that it was not true. He ended on a rhetorical high note, saying, "I did not die, I am not dying, and I will never die!" All the students exploded in laughter and the teachers had to shout at us to stop.

We had to pass an exam to be admitted to high school. Math was a joke for me, but I also enjoyed the Romanian test. We had to write a composition, and I had fun sprinkling it with neologisms, of which I only remember the word *agoraphobia* – fear of open spaces. I suppose the examiners scratched their heads trying to figure out all of them. I was on my way to high school.

AN ACCIDENTAL DISSIDENT

The Pseudo Informer

I have fond memories of my high school years. Those were years of discovery, of illumination and of desperate searches to define or redefine myself. In the middle of all these, I had some bizarre episodes of encounters with the hard edges of the totalitarian state.

I could barely wait to start the first year in high school. I remember that during the summer before the beginning of the school year, I took walks between my house and the school building, trying to imagine and feel the routine which I would repeat for the next four years. The walk from my house to the school took about forty-five minutes. I walked through the old town, with parks and historical buildings, through the medieval citadel, with its bastions, moats, cathedrals and palaces, to arrive at the school building, which was about fifty years old. Although I could have taken a bus, I preferred to walk, through good or bad weather, through the summer heat or the winter freeze, rain or snow.

***

Sometimes on my way to school and back home, I met fellow students and we walked in small groups. However, most of the time I walked alone. Those were good occasions for thinking: sometimes I tried to solve some math problem, sometimes I thought about the big questions of existence and the meaning of life, if not about a cute girl at school.

Slowly my belief in Marxism faded and was replaced by other philosophies that I encountered. While Marxism seemed to explain a great deal about nature or society, it had some serious flaws. Its prophesies about a Communist society, which would liberate and fulfill the true good nature of man, were not coming true. It promised freedom, but, as it was implemented in the Soviet Union or in Romania, it brought political prisons, censorship, and occasionally terror.

Our kind of Communism looked more like a bad joke. The top leadership of the party, the nomenklatura, were no different than a bunch of Mafia capos, who lived in luxury, defended by their lieutenants – or in this case, the whole apparatus of the state, including the feared Securitate. They were rough and boorish, with the exception of a few refined intellectuals who prostituted themselves to the regime to gain a good life and a good position. Formally, the nomenklatura did not possess riches, but the Party created a system in which they had access to the best riches of the country. They lived in huge and well-guarded villas, bought their food from a network of well-stacked Party-only stores, and had access to the best resorts in the winter or summer, reserved for them only. We had to wait in long lines to buy meat.

On the top of the pyramid was Ceauşescu himself. After he became the leader of the Communist Party, he enjoyed a brief period of relative popularity. He exposed some of the crimes of his predecessor without accusing the Party itself. The common phrase was, "some mistakes were made." It was an admission without consequence, as the same "mistakes" continued in one form or another. The second reason for his popularity was his position vis-à-vis the Soviet Union invasion of Czechoslovakia in 1968. He called a grand meeting in Bucharest, in which tens of thousands of people participated, and he delivered a televised speech in which he condemned the invasion. He, and with him all Romanians, feared that our country would also be invaded, as the Soviet leadership did not like Ceaușescu's apparent independence. After that speech, everybody thought that the times had changed, and we would evolve from the Stalinist kind of Communism to another kind, a Communism "with a human face."

The thaw did not last long. In 1970, he went to a state visit to North Korea and China, where he met Kim Il Sung and Mao. He was utterly impressed with their cult of personality. He admired the perfect discipline of their subjects and their adulation of the leader. He admired the grand performances in the large squares, in which thousands of young girls danced with flowers in perfect lines. He liked the slogans and the unison praises addressed to the great leader.

A few weeks after he returned, Ceaușescu called a meeting of the Communist party, where he formulated a new political direction for the party and country. No more flirting with decadent Western culture! From now on, movies, books, and poems must be in the spirit of proletarian socialist realism. The heroes must be the workers and the subjects must reflect their struggle to create a Communist future. They must be optimistic and inspiring. Commenting on socialist realism, a French writer once asked: "But what happens if a brick falls on the head of my hero and kills him?" The answer, at least in our case, was that bricks do not fall on the heads of the heroes. Accidents make us think about the tragedy of life, but we must all think about the great accomplishments of the Romanian people under the wise leadership of the Party.

Overnight, the whole cultural scene changed. TV programs showed Ceaușescu visiting factories and explaining to the engineers how to build factories. Public meetings ended with telegrams of congratulations to the "great leader." Publications which used to be interesting and informative were now filled with platitudes and quotes from Ceaușescu's last speeches.

Some writes and authors who desired to still publish some books of value found ways to defeat censorship. One such method was to insert some quotes from Ceaușescu's speeches in places where the subject was totally foreign to the substance of the speech. One would, for instance, publish a book about the Renaissance, and somewhere in the introduction insert something like "As comrade Nicolae Ceaușescu emphasized in his speech at the 10th Congress of the Communist Party, art must reflect the struggle of the working class and create heroes who would inspire our people to higher achievements." That was enough to mollify the censor, but everybody understood that the phrase did not come from the convictions of the author but was like a tax that must be paid to a despotic master.

Elena, Ceaușescu's wife, was promoted to higher and higher positions and later was reborn as a great scientist, researcher, and author of books on chemistry, which everybody knew that some other people wrote. There was a story circulating, according to which, in a public meeting of Romanian chemists, Elena Ceaușescu read a paper written by other researchers. She read the name of CO_2 not as carbon dioxide, but as "cotwo." Even if not true, the story illustrates what people thought about her.

We were living in the middle of a national schizophrenia. Publicly we all said the politically correct words and repeated the slogans, but privately we did not believe them. The Romanian people became, as one writer put it, "twenty million people living in the subconscious of a mad man." How could this inspire a young teenager like me?

The second reason for which I slowly abandoned Marxism was the fact that it did not answer the big questions about the meaning of life. It was all about materialism, dialectics, and class struggle. But why am I here? What is the purpose of my existence? Why is there a world instead of nothingness? Marx, Engels, or Lenin did not answer these questions.

I evolved first towards a form of atheistic existentialism. Yes, there is no God and therefore no objective, a priori meaning of life. However, it is the human being that constructs it. Existence precedes essence. Your essence is not predefined, but you build it yourself by existing, by living, by your choices, and by your deeds. If I wanted, my essence would be that of a Communist Party sycophant, but that would disgust me. At that time, my choice was to be a mathematician and a scientist, not necessarily in the outside, public, or social sense, but rather inside, as a true expression of my real essence.

***

In the ninth grade, I had for the first time the chance to participate in the national Mathematics Olympiads, which were happening every year. There was a local phase, which was all too easy, then a district phase, where I did well, and then the finals, which took place in Bucharest. A math teacher accompanied a small group of students from our district. The trip by train, which took about seven hours, was charming, as we passed through the Transylvanian hills, crossed the Southern Carpathian Mountains, and descended towards the capital. I was fascinated by the great city, the trams and the buses, the boulevards, the government buildings, and the people walking busily, strangely not aware that they were living in the greatest city of Romania.

We slept at some dormitory of a school, perhaps ten or twenty boys in a room, on metal, military style beds. In the morning, we showed up at another school and waited to start the probe, which consisted of four or five difficult math problems. As we waited outside, I carefully noticed my competitors. While I and other students from the province were shy, silent, and restrained, the students from Bucharest were laughing and talking loudly, extruding self-confidence and a sense of superiority. I did not care, as my mind was sharp and focused. As soon as I received the paper with the problems, I dived into them, forgetting myself and the world outside. We had three hours to work on them, and at the end I felt I had done a good job.

We had a day of rest, in which we went all over the city, trying to see as much as possible in the time we had. The following day, we gathered to the same school where the contest took place to receive the results. We went into a large hall, and I noticed that there were television cameras and on the podium was sitting a public figure, the academician Moisil, who was himself a mathematician and one of the pioneers of computer science in Romania. He was the one to hand the prizes to the winners.

They started with the results for the ninth grade, from the first prize, to the second, third, and then some special mentions. As the silence came over the hall, I heard my name called as the winner of the first prize for the ninth grade (together with another student from Bucharest). I walked to the podium, where the academician shook my hand and handed me the diploma and the prize consisting of a nice briefcase.

I returned to my city of Alba Iulia with an overnight train. I arrived at four in the morning and walked through the empty streets, surrounded by silence and the perfume of linden trees. My parents embraced me, and I was so happy to make them proud of me. Later I went to school, where I was congratulated by the principal and became an instant celebrity. Life was good.

I went to the math finals every year, but could not repeat the original performance, except in the twelfth grade, when I believe I got third place. I went, however, to other national finals, including physics (where I received no prize) and literature (where I remember I got some top place). I've learned one important skill from the Olympiads: how to handle defeat. After the initial success, I lost a number of times, and I was not emotionally prepared for that. A couple of times I became physically sick when the results were announced, and I did not hear my name. Later I recognized this as a stupid weakness and I was ashamed of my reaction. Defeat in the pursue of success and fame is good for one's soul.

***

I was in the eleventh grade when the school principal came during recess to tell me and another student to go to his office, where a comrade was waiting to speak with us. I

60

did as I was requested, and inside the principal's office, I met a man in his early forties. He introduced himself as a Securitate officer with the unexpected name Ceauşescu – the same last name as that of the leader of the Romanian Communist Party, "the most beloved son of the Romanian people," as our newspapers used to call him. The officer told me that he wanted to talk to me in a more private setting and he gave me a time and an address where I could meet him that same afternoon, after classes ended for the day.

The address was that of what they called a "conspiracy house", an apartment owned or rented by the Securitate, not far from my high school. I did not expect anything good to come from it, and I was concerned and curious at the same time.

I rang the bell and he received me, affable and polite. The apartment was relatively small, and it looked spartan, with minimal furniture. It was clear that no family lived there. We sat at a small table in the kitchen, which added to the air of a secrecy.

The man did not inspire me to much respect. He must have been some distant relative of the dictator, one who could easily gain position and advancement due to his name. With such a name, he did not have to be too bright to go far in life.

He was tall and well built, but with the air of a lazy guy for whom everything in life was easy. He had a large brow. well-combed black and curly hair, and pale skin which suggested he spent most of his time inside, not in the open air. I instantly associated him with a sheep. He seemed to possess some native intelligence, but not one sharpened by the effort to solve the hard questions in life.

He started by giving me a speech about patriotism and communism, about the need to defend the revolutionary accomplishments of the people from some unknown enemies. He used what we called "the wooden language," a form of speech filled with empty phrases which one could find in the propaganda articles on the first page of the Communist newspapers.

"As we know, under the leadership of the Communist Party and particularly that of comrade Nicolae Ceauşescu, Romania has made an extraordinary progress in the last decades. Now the Romanian people live at the height of human civilization. The standard of living has greatly improved, and we are lucky to live in these exciting times. At the same time, there are still elements inside and outside our country who do not like these developments and will try to create problems for us. We must always be vigilant and make sure that such elements do not hinder our progress to higher and higher peaks of civilization."

After the introduction, which seemed to be copied from the first page of the official paper of the party, he got to the point.

"We know you are a smart young man, respected by your friends and popular because of your success. We need to have more people like you. But most of all, we need you to help us guard our revolutionary conquests."

"How would I do that?" I asked, helping him to state his intention, as he circled around a little too much in preparation for the kill.

He clarified: "In essence, you will have to be our eyes and ears, to notice what goes on around you, to observe and report on any conversation or comment made by your friends and colleagues which in any way expresses doubts or opposition to the policy of the Communist Party."

He gave me an immediate test: "Maybe you can tell me right now if you have heard such talk from your colleagues."

I leaned back, looking at him, with the absent eyes of one who tries to concentrate and remember something important. I answered, "I understand perfectly what you are saying, but as I think about this, I can only tell you that all my friends are good citizens, loyal to our country and to our party. I'm happy to tell you that I have nothing to report."

He looked a little disappointed, not necessarily because he did not find this or that from me, but because my answer revealed a lack of sincerity. Everybody said something at one time or another which could be construed as being anti-party. Everybody laughed at political jokes and was happy to tell a few to his friends. It would have been so easy to remember such a joke or such a conversation and tell him about it. Instead, I adopted the same wooden language as he used. I simply stated what the newspapers were saying, that all Romanians love our party and are utterly loyal to the Genius of the Carpathians, Nicolae Ceauşescu.

He decided to let this little setback go and went for the next and final step.

"I will ask you to sign a simple paper in which you will declare that you will observe the people around you, pay attention to their words, and report anything relevant to us. Are you ready to do this?"

My mind was racing. I was not prepared for this moment; it took me by surprise. I wished somebody had warned me, maybe my own family. Some parents do not talk about sex with their children, some do not talk about such traps. My parents did not talk about either of these. I was thinking, *These guys are nuts. I can be more useful to my country, maybe even to the Communist Party, as a scientist or a researcher or an engineer. Why make me into a stooge?*

Now I had to choose.

First option: cooperate. This seemed so disgusting that the mere thought of it was making me sick. I would become a dirty rag in their hands, used for lowly tasks and discarded when not needed. I would be like an abused wife, dependent on the irrational whims of her husband, beaten, without a will of my own. I would be a Judas, betraying his best friends, and, more than that, betraying anything decent in humanity, friendship, trust, loyalty. I would be a back stabber, a man with two faces, a sick animal, a freak. All my dreams of becoming a scientist would become a joke. Can you imagine an Einstein (not that I was one, but he was an ideal) who would be informing about his friends to the German police?

Second option: refuse. However, if I refused to sign, I could see a bleak future for myself. First, I would be catalogued as an enemy, or at least an opponent of the regime. That would mean I would never be allowed to travel to the West, for instance to a scientific conference. I would not be allowed to go for a PhD, maybe not even to college. I would be spied on by some of my colleagues who agreed to sign, and denounced for the smallest sign of opposition to the Communist rule. Maybe I could become a dissident openly opposing the regime, but that was not my dream in life.

There was a third alternative, one taken by countless men and women who were forced throughout human history to go along with masters which they disapproved: appear to cooperate, but otherwise ignore, neglect, sabotage, or even betray. In my case, I would take the easiest route, that of non-performance, of failing to accomplish anything what was expected of me. Yes, I would be a total failure, a naïve ignorant who was not even capable of figuring out that some joke was political in nature and was making fun of our leader. I would be an innocent believer in the people's love for our leader, not seeing any shade of doubt in them, let alone straight opposition. I would be a yes man at the surface, but incapable of accomplishing the smallest task. In the meantime, while playing this comedy, I would pursue my real goals, living my real life in which I would be realistic, intelligent, and creative.

Yes, I would sign.

> The undersigned ... living at ... solemnly promises to inform the organs of the Securitate of any words or actions observed in my environment,

which would endanger the security of the state. I also promise not to tell anyone about my cooperation with the Securitate...

I signed and was happy to leave the apartment. A new, unhappy reality was creeping into my life, like a cancer, like a foreign body inside me, which I wanted expunged as soon as possible. Unfortunately, I could not talk to anybody about it. My mother, who was very principled, would have been too troubled, perhaps cry and not sleep. I do not know how my father would have reacted, which was making it even more dangerous. I decided to keep it to myself.

It took little time to break the promises made in the recruitment document. One fundamental aspect was that regarding secrecy - that I would not tell anybody about the fact that I was an informer. I kept that promise less than twenty-four hours. The next day, on the way to school, I met the other student who was separately called to the principal's office. I was quite sure they tried to recruit him too, and that he knew that they tried to recruit me. Were we going to regard each other with suspicion from now on? He would think I was a spy and I would think he was a spy. However, friendship was a real, fundamental thing, while the Securitate was a ghost, a daemon wandering for a short time the halls of history. I was not willing to sacrifice something real and beautiful for something false and sick.

I told my friend that the Securitate attempted to recruit me, that I formally said yes, without any serious intention to cooperate with them. "Same for me," he said. I expected that we were both going to keep quiet and not tell our recruiting officer that we talked and divulged the secret. But at the next meeting, the officer ambushed me.

66

"We know that yesterday, on the way to school, you talked with your friend. What did you tell him?" He knew something he should not have known. Suddenly, I was in danger.

***

I have asked myself many times why people agreed to be informers. Some did it for sheer fear of the recruiting officer. Some did not fear the officer, but thought that a refusal would negatively impact his life. Of these, some became productive sources of information, some drifted away, proving themselves of no value. There was another category, the worst: those who welcomed the opportunity to advance their careers or to use their position to hurt others, like the neighbor whose dog barked too much. There were also some who did it for money.

Many years after these events, I talked on Skype with a distant relative, Cornel. I was in the United States, he was in Romania. He was an interesting character, a convinced Evangelical Christian, intelligent, with a secret passion for alcohol.

"Have you read about bishop X," he asked me. "I just found out that during the Communist times he was a Secret Police informer. What a shame!"

"I did read about him," I responded, "however you have to consider some mitigating factors. First: he confessed publicly, without being unmasked by somebody. Second: he claimed that although he had signed, he never informed on anyone, which I tend to believe is true."

"No, no. Can you imagine, a bishop of the church, one who is supposed to be the shepherd leading his flock... he was in fact an informer. Shame!"

There was a pause in which he thought, and then his moral indignation took an unexpected turn.

"As a matter of fact, I was an informer myself for a while." The indignation disappeared from his tone, and now he spoke in a matter of fact style. He told me his story:

"I was recruited as an informer by one of my cousins, who was a Securitate officer. He came to me one day and, as we were enjoying some plum brandy together, he told me, 'I can fix you with some monthly stipend from Securitate. You sign to be an informer, but don't worry, you do not have to do too much. We meet a couple of times a month, and you tell me how you have heard some political jokes at a food line. Nothing substantial. They do not even have to be some new jokes or funny jokes, although to tell you the truth, my colleagues would greatly enjoy the new ones. You do not have to give me any names, just say that you have heard it from some old man, and you could not get his name. You will receive some nice money and we will have more plum brandy together.'"

"I agreed, of course, and things went well for a while... but then I got in trouble. My cousin was relocated to another city and a new control officer showed up. This one wanted real results, something more substantial. I was not happy with that, as deep inside I am not a rat."

I heard him sigh, and for a while he was silent. Then he continued.

"Fortunately, I had an idea. It was a hot summer day, one of those in which a few glasses of plum brandy really hit you hard. I bought a bottle and consumed it all by myself at home, at the same time writing a nice, professional memo to our esteemed organs of the state. Well, it may have not been too professional, for I was becoming more and more inebriated as I advanced in my composition. I set some conditions: a high base salary plus a substantial fee for every piece of information I deliver. By the time I was satisfied with my creation, I was really dizzy."

"I went to the Securitate building in town, and after entering the building, I asked in a loud voice to see the chief. I raised the paper with my hand and shouted in a loud voice that these are my demands for cooperation. Some officers came to talk to me and looked at me like I was sick, until they got tired of me and literally threw me out in the street. That was the end of my service with the Securitate."

***

I bumbled something about some insignificant conversation with my friend. I was not a good liar anyway, and if the officer were smart enough, he could have easily concluded that I was hiding something. Whatever it was, he tried to keep the conversation friendly. He was not giving up on me and kept asking about anything that I might have seen or heard. In response to all his questions about my friends and colleagues, I continued to claim that they were all good communists who loved the country and the party and that nobody was ever saying anything about them. Highly incredible!

He then tried another angle:

"Do you know Elena H. from the class XI B?"

She was a popular girl, attractive, who considered boys her age much too immature, with the possible exception of some soccer players who were equally popular. She went out with older guys who had long since finished high school. Of course, I knew her, and I acknowledged it.

"What can you tell me about her?" he asked.

"Unfortunately, not too much. I am not part of her circle of friends."

"Have you noticed she has a cosmopolitan appearance and cosmopolitan attitudes?"

Cosmopolitan was bad, at least from the point of view of the Communist Party. A cosmopolitan person admired the West, and consequently suffered from Western influences. A young cosmopolitan teenager might listen to Beatles at Radio Free Europe and inevitably swallow some capitalist propaganda on the side. A cosmopolitan young person could wear Western style dress, purchased from some foreigners, with whom he or she might have carried dangerous conversations.

"What do you mean by cosmopolitan?" I asked innocently.

"For instance, she wears blue jeans," he explained. "Have you noticed? Have you seen her on the street, wearing blue jeans?"

I faked some concentration as if I had to recall something. Then my face lighted with a smile. "Yes, I do remember now. I am sure I saw her wearing blue jeans." ... just as many other young people wear blue jeans, I might have added.

Now he was getting somewhere with me. "Are you sure you have not heard her saying something of interest?"

"No, no," I protested, "I certainly would have told you if I did."

He could not let it go and he was determined to show some progress with me.

"Are you ready to write a note stating that you have noticed her cosmopolitan attitudes, including wearing blue jeans?"

"Yes," I answered, "I can certainly state that she was wearing jeans. As to the cosmopolitan attitudes, I am not sure, not knowing her well enough. I will just state the facts, but you can draw any conclusions you want."

I wrote an "informative note":

> I, the undersigned… would like to state that I
> have seen Elena H., student at the HCC High
> School, wearing jeans on the streets of our city. I

have also seen her entering a local café with some of her friends.

I signed and gave him the paper, hoping he would be satisfied and leave me alone. Perhaps encouraged by this small progress in developing me as a source of precious information, he proposed another meeting.

We met at the same apartment, where he continued to press me for information, trying to stimulate my memory in various ways. "What about your colleague X? What about Y? What was discussed at that party?" … and so on. To his disappointment, I was only remembering good things about my friends.

Suddenly I had an idea. I could give him something real.

"In fact, comrade captain, I do remember now something of high importance, something regarding our state secrets."

"You do!" he exclaimed with joy and settled himself in a new position on the chair, ready for some long story.

"Here is what happened," I started. "I was travelling by train from Alba Iulia to Bucharest. The train was slowing to pull in to a station, when I noticed a sign that read NO PHOTOGRAPHY. Must have been some military installation, or weapons factory, or something of that kind, I cannot say. To my surprise, exactly at that moment when I saw the sign, a man moved to the window, pulled out a camera, and took a picture. It was quite obvious."

I leaned back, savoring my victory. The enemy of the state was unmasked! My controller looked pleased. His efforts were about to produce some substantial results, which might translate into a significant boost for his career. All he had to do now was to exploit the information in a professional manner, as it was fit for a Securitate officer. Perhaps a series of smart questions would develop this into a real case.

"Who was the man who took the pictures?"

"Unfortunately, I did not know him, so I cannot say."

"What did he look like? How was he dressed?"

"I wish I would answer that, but I can't. This happened five years ago, when I was going to a summer camp. I was, as you can understand, much younger, just a child, so my memory is somewhat vague. However, I am absolutely sure that I saw the No Photography sign and that I saw the man taking pictures, no doubt about it. I immediately recognized that he was doing something wrong, so that registered in my memory."

He did not give up and tried another angle.

"In which city or town did this happen? At what train stop?"

"I am ashamed to tell you I cannot remember that either," I responded. "I was just a child, thirteen years old... In any case, do you want me to write an information note about this?"

"No, not at this time… perhaps if you remember more."

He was obviously disoriented. I wish I knew what went through his mind. Did he think I was stupid or that I was making fun of him? Regardless, he did not ask me for another secret meeting, and with that, my career as a confidential informer came to a sudden and pathetic end.

***

During summer vacations I worked various jobs. For a few weeks, I was a vendor at a street book stand. I got the job through the mother of a friend, who was the manager of the city's largest bookstore. (This was one of the advantages of living in a small city, where everybody knew everybody.) As I was paid on commission, the store manager and I played a little outside the rules. I told all my acquaintances to remember me when they intended to buy a book. If I could not sell it to them because it was not in my inventory, they would tell me that the book was in the store, and my manager would transfer it to me, so I could make a commission from the sale. I was zealous, selling books to everybody, whether they needed them or not. When my sister gave birth to her first child, I saw my brother-in-law who was on his way to the hospital to see his wife and baby, and I tricked him into buying a bunch of books about caring for newborns. I suppose he will not be angry with me after such a tremendous event.

I really liked my job at the Hydrologic Institute, which had an office in our city. My father was a good friend of the office chief. My duty was to travel by bike to various locations around the city and take readings of the level of water from specially built fountains, consisting of pipes going deep into the ground. The readings were sent to Bucharest, where scientists and engineers used them to predict the movement of underground water, and ultimately the possibility of floods.

I would leave the office on a summer day to visit all the locations on my list. I would stop at a location, take a reading, then sit down and read from a book for the next hour. Sometimes I took rest at the edge of a river, enjoying the smells of the fields and the singing of the birds. The next day I would visit other locations.

On a few occasions, I spent too much time reading or resting, and I missed some locations, which was a serious dereliction of duty. I found a solution. I would try to find a mathematical function that would approximate well the evolution of water levels in the last two weeks and then use the function to extrapolate the level on the day I failed to measure it. There was my number. Fortunately, no catastrophic floods happened at that time.

***

During my school years, I was occasionally infatuated with one girl or another. There was a Mihaela in the second grade and an Angela in the third, then another Mihaela in the seventh grade. I was then in love with two other girls with musical names, Dorela and Mirela, the syllables in their names denoting notes in the musical scale.

My experience with Mirela was the most painful one and happened in the summer before first year of high school. While she did not even know, I was so in love with her that I felt sick and could not eat. I passed daily in front of her house, hoping to see her, and a few times I succeeded, but I did not dare say more than a few words. Then one day, a disaster: I saw her in the cinema hall with another boy, older than me. I described my pain to my best friend at that time, Sorin, and he suggested we catch the boy in some corner and give him a thrashing when nobody was looking. I declined his proposal.

When school started, I wanted to talk to her but lacked the courage. Eventually I swallowed my fear, and during a break between classes, I went to her and told her, perhaps with an unnatural voice distorted by emotion, that I wanted to be her friend. She looked at me as if I came from another planet, then said, "Sure," turned her back, and left. I did not dare approach her again, but within a week I discovered other interests and forgot her completely.

Only in the last two years of high school I became more relaxed. I had a girlfriend in the twelfth grade, Felicia. This time, we spent time together, took long walks, held hands, and maybe even kissed.

***

The memory of my shame in middle school, when the principal scolded the Baptist students and I declared that I did not believe in God, was still looming in my mind. I was very afraid that there would be a repeat of this in high school, and I was not sure how I would react this time. After winning first prize at the national level of the Mathematics Olympiad, I did not believe any teacher or principal would attempt to humiliate me publicly. I was an asset to my school, which after my performance decided to start a new educational track, the Special Mathematics track, separate from the others, Real, Humanities and Classic. In spite of all this, it could still happen, most likely not because of some school initiative, but because of some directive coming from above, which the school would have to obey.

I had no solution for my moral dilemma. How would I respond if I were publicly unmasked as a Baptist? I could deny it, saying I did not believe in God – which was the truth – but then I would appear as a weakling unable to come out of his mother's control. Worse, word would travel, and my mother would find out. I was not afraid of her, but I loved her and felt sorry for her. She was a woman who already experienced suffering and rejection in her life. She had lost her mother when she was four years old, then, in her first marriage, she ended up with a cheating husband whom she had to leave. Now I was her only son, her joy, her pride, her hope. If she heard that I denied God and denied her, she would be utterly ruined.

Unmasked as a Baptist, I could also stand on my feet and say, "Yes, I'm a Christian," but that would be a lie. Even worse, they could try to humiliate me and put pressure on me to give up my faith. I would be thrown in a battle which was not my own.

Inside I disagreed with my mother's faith, but I loved and respected her. I agreed with the official atheism, but I despised our authorities who promoted it. I did not think about this dilemma every day, but I had a continuous worry somewhere in the back of my mind, an expectation of an imminent disaster.

My biology classes kept bringing this conflict to my conscience. All teachers had some nicknames invented by the students, and our biology teacher was called The Spitter, as he had a tendency to throw little bubbles of saliva when he spoke, especially when he got emotional. He used any occasion to talk about the superiority of science over religion. When he talked about science, he used one type of voice, when he talked about religion, another. Science was the domain of intelligent human beings, in which humanity was rising to new heights. Religion was the domain of ignorant, stupid, and uneducated people. From there, he moved into mockery. He told us jokes in which Christians in general, and Baptists in particular, were ridiculed. While nobody in the class reacted, he broke into laughter and enjoyed himself. He was unique in that respect, as most of our other teachers were decent and, I suppose, believed in God secretly but could not state it publicly.

I developed a dislike of him and enjoyed every opportunity in which he was disrespected by the students. One time, we had a lesson about human reproduction, and he seemed to have a special satisfaction in presenting himself as a liberated human being, free from the inhibitions and taboos still present in our families. At the end, he said,

"Now is the time to ask any question you ever had about sex. I know that you are afraid to talk to your parents about this, but you can ask me. Come on, don't be shy. I see you girls giggling there, I'm sure you know a lot about this subject. Ha, ha, ha. Please, ask any question."

My best friend, who was sitting next to me, raised his hand.

"You there, go ahead, don't be shy."

"Comrade teacher, I have had this question in my mind for a long time, but I did not know how to ask. The question is this: how does the human embryo eliminate its excrements?"

The class exploded in laughter and the teacher froze while the superior smile disappeared from his face. He blinked nervously a number of times.

"Are you mocking me?" he said in a threatening voice. "Are you mocking me? How dare you?"

"Sorry, sir," my friend answered, faking surprise and confusion. "You told us we could ask any question."

"You should go and ask your own mother how you eliminated excrements in her belly!" the teacher exploded in frustration.

The laughter grew even more. Fortunately for everybody, the bell rang. The teacher took his notes and went towards the door with his head up, as a sign of preserving his dignity. At the door he turned back and said, "You want war, you'll have war!" Then he stepped out, slamming the door.

Nothing bad came out of the incident, but I heard that some other teachers heard about it and had a good laugh. I had my secret satisfaction.

***

When I was in the twelfth grade, during the winter, our geography teacher organized a trip to Budapest. It was exciting, as trips to foreign countries were not common, and permission to travel was rarely granted and only to trusted citizens. Unreliable people, dissidents or criminals were never allowed to step out of the country. Normal people who did not have a "bad file," were occasionally allowed to travel to socialist countries like Hungary or Bulgaria. Yugoslavia was more difficult, as it was more liberal and offered more opportunities to escape to the West. Next came the capitalist countries, for which only the most reliable and verified people got passports and visas. Later, when I was in college, I was invited once to a house party by a girl whose parents were high in the Party hierarchy, and she showed us a movie they made during a visit to London. I was amazed that somebody could go as a tourist to a capitalist country, in the same way in which we, ordinary people, were able to visit some city in Romania.

Visiting another country, even if only our neighbor Hungary, was an exciting opportunity. I would see not just a beautiful capital city, but I would also step into another world, in a new way of existence. It was almost like visiting heaven. Many of my friends were interested in going shopping, as Hungary was known as a more consumerist-friendly country, but I wanted to see the roads, the bridges, the buildings, and the people. Budapest was a destination for many Romanians during the time of the Austria-Hungarian Empire, and I would perhaps walk through the same streets and see the same images as some of our Transylvanian compatriots, who were there as students or engineers or diplomats. I would perhaps walk where my grandfather once walked, on his way to the First World War battle of Galicia.

The plan was to leave Alba Iulia early in the morning by bus and travel to Oradea, the Romanian city next to the border with Hungary. We would stay at a school dormitory, then enter Hungary immediately after midnight and return immediately before the next midnight, thus maximizing the time allowed for the approved one-day trip.

In the morning, we gathered at a location in the city, where the bus was waiting, and boarded the bus. We had to wait for a few minutes for a "collective passport" document to be delivered to our geography teacher, which was an official list with the participants of the trip that were allowed to cross the border. Finally, the document arrived, and as our teacher scanned it, he noticed that the number of people on the list was one fewer than the number of people on the bus. One name was missing. He read the names out loud to discover who was omitted. My name was the one missing.

"There must be something wrong, some mistake," he said. "Let me call the Securitate number and try to correct it."

He tried but could not find anybody to help. The whole group was waiting just because of me. He made the decision to leave, promising to call back from the road and somehow get a corrected list after we arrived in Oradea. He was genuinely concerned about me, as I was almost part of his family, being the best friend of his son for many years.

We arrived in Oradea and he made more calls, but to no avail. Eventually, late in the evening, as the bus was being prepared for the next stage of the trip, the teacher told me that he had no choice but to leave me behind. I was to stay at the dormitory, spend a day alone in Oradea, then be picked up by the group when they would return.

All my friends boarded the bus, filled with excitement for what lay ahead. After a few minutes, the noise disappeared to be replaced by silence and loneliness. Strangely enough, while I was disappointed in how things turned out, I was neither depressed nor angry. The silence of an empty building was an invitation to meditation and reflection on the important things in life. While my friends were enlarging their horizontal space, I was enlarging my inner space. It made me feel special.

I awoke early in the morning, got dressed, closed the doors of the building with the key they left me, and went to explore the city. It was still dark and freezing cold, perhaps one of the coldest days of the year. I was not properly dressed for that kind of weather, and soon, despite waking fast, I started to feel the bitter cold. I found, however, that the mind can conquer the harsh conditions to which the body is subjected. I had just read a great book, *Narcissus and Goldmund* by the German author Herman Hesse, and I remembered an episode in which the main hero, Goldmund, is crossing some deserted fields in the middle of the winter. Goldmund had run from a monastery and wandered medieval Europe, going from city to city and from village to village, occasionally sleeping with some peasant wife he found in the fields. He was my hero. Eventually he returned to the monastery, but found that it was not for him, so he left for the last time. A blizzard started, and he was lost in fields and forests, a lonely man walking for days through bitter cold and darkness. He had visions of mythical fairies ripping his flesh, and eventually died. I expected to see the beautiful fairies biting me, but it did not happen. After a few hours of waking alone through the streets of the city, I got tired and thought of a more practical outcome.

I remembered that my mother had given me the address of a cousin of hers who lived in the city of Oradea. At around eight in the morning, I headed to the address I had written on a scrap of paper. I arrived unannounced but was received with warmth and joy. My mother's cousin had two daughters my age - my second cousins. One was sixteen, one was eighteen, and they were both beautiful and friendly and happy to meet their second cousin for the first time in their lives. The younger one was especially attractive, and I was amused to hear that she was trying to make up her mind between becoming a model or a nuclear physicist. Perhaps the first career suited her better.

I had a substantial breakfast with them, then they took me out. We wandered through the city for many hours, visiting parks and museums, then returned for a fabulous dinner. In the evening, I went back to the dorm to wait for the bus to return with my fellow students from Budapest. They arrived at midnight, carrying bags filled with Western goods, from bottles of Coca Cola to clothes or small radio sets. Everybody was excited and continued to talk late into the night. In the morning, we boarded the bus and left for our home city of Alba Iulia. My girlfriend Felicia was laughing and joking with all the others on the way home, and suddenly I felt that we were emotionally disconnected from one another, that we belonged to different worlds, and so I lost interest in her.

I could not stop asking myself why I was singled out and not allowed to cross into Hungary. I could not figure it out at that time, but now I believe I know: it was a consequence of my poor performance as an informer.

Perhaps the Securitate captain was scolded by his superiors for his failure to develop me into a proper informer, and he took his revenge on me by crossing out my name.

***

A bizarre episode with political overtones happened to us in March of our senior year of high school, a few months before graduation.

Ceauşescu was initially the First Secretary of the Central Committee of the Romanian Communist Party. He did not like that title, so they changed it to General Secretary. He was at the same time the President of the Council of State, and that was not good enough for him either. He decided to be the President of Romania, a more glorious title.

There was to be a ceremony for him to receive the title and the symbols of the position, which included a golden scepter. With the title and the scepter, he would look more like the glorious kings from our past, like Michael the Brave or Stephan the Great. Only fools would take that seriously. In reality, he was a shrewd peasant from the Oltenia, a southern province of Romania, with little education and a narrow mind which could not break out of the patterns ingested in his Communist education in Moscow. This made him the target of political jokes carefully shared between close friends.

The whole country was supposed to be in total awe at this generous gift of Fate who gave us such an illustrious man. Meetings were organized all over the country which ended with the usual resolution expressing happiness about the event and thanking the Communist Party and Ceaușescu personally for leading us to happy times, the most glorious in the history of our country.

The day of the investiture ceremony was a special day in our high school, and I suppose in all schools. Normal classes were suspended, and we were gathered in a large room, teachers and students, to watch the ceremony live on TV. A teacher gave a short speech before it started, and everybody applauded, while nobody believed one bit of what was said. While Ceaușescu received the scepter, we were supposed to be totally transfixed as if we were having a divine vision.

As the ceremony unfolded, two of my friends found a dark corner where they started to play cards, oblivious to the crucial event that was supposed to change history. They did not expect to be seen, or – worst case – if they were, to be gently admonished by some teacher. Unfortunately for them and all of us, they were noticed by a crazy inspector from the Education Department of the city. When he saw them, he went berserk. He could barely control himself enough to wait for the end of the televised live event, after which he exploded with rage and hate. His face was red, and his eyes were bulging.

"You are criminals! You are that kind of young people from whom assassins of presidents are recruited! You scum! I will immediately report this outrage to Securitate. You will be arrested and thrown in prison, where you will spend the rest of your miserable lives!" … and he went on and on for a long time.

Behind the falsely penitent faces of the students and the falsely severe faces of the teachers, I was sure that everybody was thinking, "Is this man mad? Is this guy an idiot? What does he want?"

The school principal felt obliged to say something, and he certainly could not defend the two students. Yes, what they did was an outrage. He admonished them, told them they should be ashamed and that he will make sure they will be severely punished. We left disgusted, waiting for the blade of the guillotine to fall soon.

The next day, we were told that there would be a meeting of students, teachers and parents, in which this serious offence would be discussed. Any missing parents would risk the expulsion of their children. The verdict and sentence would be announced at that time. Waiting for the meeting, we, the students, joked about the whole situation and cursed the mad inspector.

The day came, and we were all assembled in our classroom. The inspector was not present, which brought all of us a sigh of relief. One teacher welcomed the parents and said we were all good students and that if we worked well we would have a a great future. Then the principal spoke, chastised the students guilty of irreverence to the "most beloved son of our people," but he spoke more like a parent than a prosecutor. One of our colleagues also spoke, and he emphasized that while some mistake was made (that was the phrase used to characterize some of the worst crimes of the regime), the whole thing was misunderstood, as we all love the school, the teachers, the country, the Communist Party and have great love and respect for our leader, comrade Nicolae Ceaușescu.

What started with a bang, ended with a whisper. I believe all who were present there understood that we had to go through the motions to appease the Securitate and the local Communist organization. I felt sympathy for the teachers and even for our school principal. They were good people, and while playing the role of loyal Communists, they did not go so far as to punish the political offense. Not everybody could be a hero, but most people could at least remain decent.

The whole episode was over, and we never heard about it after that. There were no negative consequences for the two colleagues who committed the crime of *lèse-majesté*. They went to college, graduated, married and otherwise had normal lives.

***

I graduated in 1974. For graduation, we had to go through an exam called Baccalaureate, which covered the main subjects taught in high school, such as math, physics, Romanian language and literature, and social sciences. I passed all subjects with the maximum possible grade.

Next, I went to Bucharest for the entrance exams of the Faculty of Mathematics at the University of Bucharest. I could have gone to Cluj, which was a beautiful Transylvanian city, cultured, with an old history and close to my home (about 80 miles), but I chose to go to the more prestigious University of Bucharest for a three main reasons. One of them was to be farther of my parents and thus reduce the stress due to the tension between my atheistic beliefs and my mother's faith. Sooner or later, my parents would know that I did not believe in God, but it would be easier if I were far away. The second reason was that I wanted to live in another culture than that of the one in Transylvania, where I grew up. It was like moving from a small, civilized, and friendly Ohio town to the toughness of New York. I was hungry for life and adventure. I was somewhat fascinated by the Balkan culture after reading the poetry of Ioan Barbu, who was both a poet and mathematician. His poems depicted Turkish cafes with old and fat prostitutes waiting for clients to show up, but surprisingly, the poet succeeded in mixing such images with beautiful mathematical structures. The third reason was that Bucharest was recognized as having the best and most prestigious Mathematics Faculty at the University of Bucharest.

The entrance exams were held in July, and it just happened that Bucharest was experiencing one of the hottest summers in history. The asphalt of the sidewalk was soft and melting, as the temperatures rose to over 40 Celsius (107 Fahrenheit). I had a small room in some acquaintances' apartment, and without air conditioning at that time, I kept the window open and was covered in sweat as I laid almost naked on the bed. Despite this small annoyance, I felt happy and fulfilled.

There were five exams I had to pass - three were written exams, the others oral - and I passed all of them with the maximum grade of 10. At the oral exam, the professors already knew the results of the written tests and knew of me from the Mathematics Olympiads where I took top places, so they did not bother to ask many questions. It was rather an enjoyable discussion on some of the subjects and of my intentions regarding my future career in math.

After scoring the perfect 10, I returned home, ready for the next step in life, the military, which was mandatory at that time in Romania. Students who passed the college entrance exams were supposed to go through a "reduced term" training, lasting only nine months, as opposed to the 18 months for other young men.

A few days after I returned, I met a lady who lived across the street and had two sons who were college students in Cluj. She was protective of them, and when they went to their entrance exams, she accompanied them, taking with her money and gifts to oil their way into college. She asked me if I passed the exams, and when I answered in the affirmative, she drew closer to me and asked in a conspiratorial voice, "Did your parents bribe some professor to insure you pass?" I said no, it was not necessary. Then she smiled and patted me on the shoulder, saying, "I know you are a proud boy and do not want to acknowledge it, but I am sure your parents did." I did not argue. As they say, a thief thinks everybody is a thief.

The Convert

On a September night, I was riding on a train with two other guys towards the city of Slatina to report to the artillery regiment, where we were to perform our military duties. The rule was this: all boys at the age of 18 or 19 were supposed to enter military service for eighteen months, but the ones who were admitted to college only had to stay half the time, for nine months. These boys received training to become future reserve officers. They graduated as sergeants after these nine months, and were supposed to perform additional training during the college years, then receive a commission as junior lieutenants after graduation from college.

It would not be original for me to express the opinion that military service is beneficial for young men, and it was beneficial for me in particular. It was a big change from home, where my mother prepared all meals and my family surrounded me with love and care. Now I found a sergeant shouting at me that being hungry or tired or cold is one of the rigors of military life.

I will only relate a few stories, which I find relevant for this narrative.

We had, in turn, a number of commanders, among them a major who won our hearts. Because he was loved and respected, we obeyed all rules of military discipline out of affection for him. Every month, we had a meal together with the officers in which we were served not only good food but also vodka, something not allowed to our

American counterparts of the same age. After one of these events, the major sat with us and we had an informal discussion.

He told us – to my surprise – that there was no expectation we would ever fight NATO, despite this being the official line. Our manuals described the NATO military organization and the weapons they would use in case of war.

"Who then is our expected enemy?" we asked.

"Our great neighbor to the north," responded the major. That was the Soviet Union, the senior partner in our Warsaw Treaty Alliance.

Interesting. The expectation was that we would turn against our closest ally, for which we otherwise had no love. Romania had a long history of switching alliances. We were with the Turks against the Austrians, then with the Russians against the Turks, then with the French and British against Germany, then with Germany against Russia, then with Russia against Germany. There was no shame in this. We were a small country, and our only hope for survival was in playing the big powers against each other and siding with the most powerful, as long as they offered us some protection. We would not die for the greater glory of Nazism or Communism.

"But how could we fight them?" we asked. "They are so much stronger than us."

"Our strategy," the major explained, "is to hold and not be overrun for two weeks. If we succeed, chances are that other big powers would get into a conflict and our enemy, whoever it is, will have some more pressing priorities than to defeat us."

I came to know the life of a soldier, which was divided between periods of boredom and intense activity. Unless we were tired, in the evenings we had time to read, play cards or talk. We formed a math club, where we discussed advanced math and challenged each other with interesting but difficult problems. We discussed literature, philosophy, and occasionally politics. I was surprised to find that I had peers who actually believed in Communism, not so much as a theory but as a system which benefits the people. No wonder: in this case, "the people" consisted of their families, who were well placed in the system.

In our TR battalion (TR stands for Reduced Term, the order of words being reversed in Romanian), we had a few guys who came from the middle layers of the Nomenklatura, the top echelon of the Communist Party. There were no special privileges for them, except the fact that they received passes for a two- or three-day visit home before the rest of us. When some guy received the pass, we asked how he managed to get it. "My father has a friend who has a cousin who is a General at the Ministry of Defense" was the usual answer.

My father tried to arrange that for me too, and it worked, but in strange circumstances. He had a friend who had a sister who was a tailor in Slatina, the place of our regiment. She was well-placed, as many officers of the regiment came to her for her tailoring services. She knew some of the higher ranks and it was easy for her to ask an officer the favor of giving me a pass, for the promise to finish his wife's dress a few days earlier.

92

One morning in January, we were waiting outside in formation in the rain, while a major whom we called Torquemada (after the Great Inquisitor) was inspecting our dormitories. Suddenly, another soldier came outside of the dormitory and called my name. I went inside, expecting some trouble.

"Oara," the major said, "can you confirm that you were this morning in charge of the washing room?"

"Yes, comrade major," I responded.

"What were your duties?"

"To leave everything sparkling clean."

"Then how do you explain this?" he asked, then he showed me some traces of mud, left by somebody's boots.

The explanation was simple. After I cleaned the washing room, we all went out in the courtyard, but somebody needed to visit the toilet and went back in. It was rainy and muddy outside, so no wonder the floor had traces of mud.

"Comrade major, allow me to explain…" I started.

At that point, the major abandoned the tone of a smart detective and started to shout: "Soldier, I do not want to hear excuses, I want an explanation for this serious dereliction of duty! Why is the floor dirty with mud?"

I tried again: "Comrade major, please allow me to answer."

His face became red, he interrupted me again and raised his voice even higher. "No! No! No! … I do not want to hear stupid excuses. I want to know why is the floor dirty?"

This time I shut up. I realized that there was no point in giving an honest answer. He wanted to find some victim to show his toughness, so there I was, a most convenient victim. I became silent, as if I was guilty and intimidated, without anything to say.

Now he was satisfied. His voice went back to normal and he said:

"Here is your punishment. Saturday morning you report to the guard's building for a one-day arrest."

I was not troubled. Some of my companions told me that I would not become a real man without at least one day of arrest. I was ready to become a real man.

To my surprise, on that Friday evening, a lieutenant colonel came to our unit and asked for me. When I showed up, he gave me a paper and explained that it was a three days pass to go home and visit my family.

"Unfortunately, I have been punished with a day arrest, and I have to show up for it tomorrow," I said with regret.

He shrugged. "Don't worry. Just go. This paper is all you need."

The next day, I dressed up and went to the train station, but not directly. I was afraid that I would meet some military police patrol which would stop me. They might have had the list of people who were supposed to show up for arrest, in which case they would have returned me to the barracks in spite of my papers.

For the first time in my life, I felt like a chased animal. I was shrewd and careful. All my senses were sharp, and as I moved through the streets, I calculated at each moment what I would do if I encountered the military police. At this place I would jump over a fence and hide. At that place I would turn the corner and run. I was determined to do whatever necessary to reach the train station. When I finally arrived there, I stayed in a dark corner and jumped in the train at the last moment, after the train started to move. It was good training for the future, although I did not know it at that time.

I was in general a quiet man and respectful of authority, but I found that not everybody was like that. One Sunday evening, in the spring, one of our guys from our TR unit came into the dorm and said, "Guys, tomorrow we'll have some fun. I went into the city without a pass and I spent some good time at a bar. When I was coming out, I met face-to-face with our commander, Torquemada, and we made eye contact. I think he was too surprised to say anything, so I made believe I did not see him and just walked. Watch what will happen tomorrow morning at formation time."

The name of the fellow was Toma. He was from the city of Constanța, at the Black Sea. He had a dark complexion, a black mustache, and looked more like a Levantine smuggler, which fitted him well, as a lot of

95

smuggling was happening in the port. I am sure he had a lot of practice avoiding the police, which explains his coolness.

The next morning, as we were standing at attention in formation, Torquemada approached us with a satisfied grin on his face. Sure of himself, he asked for Toma to step in front of the formation, then, not looking at him, but at the rest of us, he asked:

"Soldier, where were you yesterday at 3 PM?"

Toma was a calm as he could be.

"I was at in the dorm, comrade major."

Torquemada blinked his eyes a couple of times, as if to recover from some misunderstanding.

"No, soldier, I mean Sunday at 3 PM."

"I respectfully confess that I was in the dorm, reading a book."

"You are lying! How dare you lie to my face?"

"Comrade major, I'm telling you the absolute truth. You can even ask my fellow soldiers, they saw me around all day."

"Soldier Toma, one of us is a fool!" exclaimed in frustration Torquemada. "Go back in formation and try to remember better."

Nothing came out of it, but I realized that I and Toma were made of a different material. I would have been afraid and perhaps immediately confessed to the crime of leaving the unit without a pass, accepting the consequences. Here was this young man, totally calm, ready to lie without the smallest hesitation.

***

My existential crisis started as soon as I finished the military service and came home, in mid-June. While vacation was usually a time of fun, I remember that summer as one of unhappiness.

At that time, I had already gone through a number of philosophies or worldviews. I used to believe in God with a child's faith, but I lost that faith at around the age of twelve.

For a while I believed in science and Marxism (which was supposed to be "scientific"), but I gave it up disgusted by the reality of communism and by the failure to answer some important questions in life. It was a theory about history and society, but it did not tell me anything personally. After that I turned to atheistic existentialism, developed by French thinkers like Sartre or Camus. Later I found it too subjective, far from logic and science. More like the musings of some neurotic people. For a while I felt attracted by logical positivism, which had the advantage of being closer to math and science. It had some artificial rigor, by rejecting any questions related to poorly defined concepts, such as life, love, or purpose, which could not be described using the terminology of science. Questions related to the meaning of life were meaningless. In the end, this did not satisfy me. It was not that I thought of myself as smarter than Marxists or Existentialists or Positivists, but their philosophy did not resonate with me anymore, so I was in search of something else.

I was now in no-man's land, not sure where to go and what to believe. I was living with a contradiction which I could not resolve. On one hand, mathematics gave me access to a world which was perfect, beautiful, rational, and logical. On the other hand, the world of man, society, politics, as well as my own life was filled with imperfections, failures and lies. Why this gap? Was it possible to find moral beauty and truth in the world of humans? Was there any grand unifying principle which could explain both and, most importantly, transcend the misery of the human existence?

I started to get some glimpses of a solution by following the stories of Russian dissidents on Radio Free Europe. There was Solzhenitsyn, who wrote books containing the truth about the life in the Communist USSR. He was threatened, imprisoned, and bullied, but he continued to speak the truth and was eventually expelled from the Soviet Union in 1974, the previous year. There were other Russian dissidents, including the physicist Andrei Sakharov. For me, they shone like diamonds in a pile of garbage. In their fearless standing for truth, they possessed some of the beauty and rigor of mathematics.

That summer, I saw two movies which further showed me that it was possible to live in truth and uphold human dignity inside an oppressive political system.

In the movie *Becket*, the main character takes his responsibility as a church bishop seriously, getting into a conflict with the king. His stand was even more impressive because he was once a friend of the king, participating together in various acts of debauchery before being appointed to a high position in the Church. He did not hate the king, but considered his duty to God and Church to be of a higher order. He stood tall in a world in which everything conspired to make him bend. Eventually, the king utters the famous words, "Will no one rid me of this turbulent priest?" The king's nobles understood and responded by killing Becket.

The second movie was *A Man for All Seasons*, with a similar story. Thomas More stood on his principles and refused to approve of the king's decision to divorce his wife and marry Anne Boylan. All kinds of pressures are brought against him, but he did not relent. I could relate to Thomas More because, like me, he was not a naturally courageous man. At one point he said, "When God puts me in a difficult position to defend His truth, I try to hide and avoid the danger as much as I can. But when God pushes me to a corner from where I cannot avoid it any more, I ultimately chose to be on his side." Just like Becket, Thomas More ended up losing his life.

Why could people like Becket and More live by the truth and proclaim the truth, risking their lives, while I was surrounded by people who joined in praising Communism and praising Ceaușescu. Forced to do it, I was myself publicly proclaiming the lies, as I was afraid and did not want to compromise my future.

The common line which I found in all these heroes was faith. They believed in something that was higher than themselves, something that gave them strength. Their lives had meaning, because the meaning was coming from a higher order of reality. If all existence is limited to matter, energy and chance, to the survival of the fittest, then resistance is futile. I could survive better by proclaiming the lies and being part of a corrupt system.

A new worldview started to emerge in my mind. Proper meaning, truth, and morals can only be sustained if there is a higher being, God. Humanity had some degree of perfection but suffered a catastrophic fall into moral disease and misery. Perhaps this disease can be corrected by reconnecting to God. All these thoughts brought me closer to the Christian worldview, but I was not yet ready to accept it.

As I prepared for my first year of college, I had a plan. Being far from my parents, I would gradually stop attending church. Even if I went to church a couple of times to mollify my mother, I was in less danger to be discovered in Bucharest, which was a city larger than Alba Iulia by orders of magnitude. To lower the impact, I would leave some small room for change, so there would not be a traumatic break which would lead my mother to despair. It looked like a fundamental problem in my life was about to be solved in time.

On a September day, I took the train to Bucharest, carrying with me the heavy luggage with clothes to last me through the fall and winter. I arrived at Gara de Nord, the main train station, from where I took a bus to the student dorms. Some of my army buddies were already there, and after I settled, we went together to explore the city.

The first day of school was on a Monday, but on Sunday I decided to go visit some Baptist churches in the city. That was contrary to my great plans, but consistent with my spiritual search. The churches were known by the streets where they resided, so in the morning I went to the Titulescu church on Nicolae Titulescu Boulevard. I was not impressed, but I decided to try again in the afternoon, going to the Mihai Bravu church on the Mihai Bravu Boulevard.

This time it was different. The man who preached was not a professional cleric, but an engineer, Aurel Popescu. Perhaps because of his education and formation, he spoke my language, and I followed his sermon with great interest. While I do not remember exactly the subject, somehow he touched exactly the issues in which I was interested. The main point I retained after listening to him was that the solution to humanity's poor state was called salvation and it came through Jesus Christ. That was the moment when I decided that Christianity is true and real, and that I wanted to be a Christian.

I talked to Aurel Popescu at the end of the service, telling him about my struggles and the decision to believe in Jesus Christ. He gave me some advice, and he also invited me to visit his home, where Christians often met for discussions, study, and prayer. I accepted his invitation, which proved to have major consequences for my future.

After that eventful Sunday, I started my first day in college on Monday morning. I was where I wanted to be, in a school where I did not have to bother with chemistry, biology, or literature, and I could savor mathematics at the fullest. I considered myself lucky to spend all day attending lectures, studying, and solving the problems we received as homework. I immersed myself in study with enthusiasm and joy. The more challenging a particular subject was, the better. Algebra was my main interest, and when the professor gave us a list of 120 problems and asked each one of us to pick five, I fought to take the most difficult ones, which I was able to solve without too much effort.

While I was enjoying my first days of college, I started to regularly attend the Mihai Bravu church. We had two services every Sunday and one service in the middle of the week. Between school and church, I took long strolls to the parks, while my mind was racing to rethink everything about life, faith, and science.

Many years later, when I was working as a software developer, I found a good metaphor for that period in my life. In developing software, sometimes one must "refactor" the code. Refactoring consists of rearranging and reorganizing the already existing code in new ways, making it cleaner, better architected, and more suitable for future developments. The developer cuts some programs into smaller units, joins some smaller units into larger ones, makes the code more generic, elegant, and flexible. This is what I was doing with my mind on that September. I spend hours rethinking various concepts and rearranging them in new categories. It was like when a scientist makes a breakthrough discovery, after which he realigns everything to fit into a completely new frame. Suddenly everything starts making sense, in the light of the new concepts. This is what some people call a paradigm shift.

***

For the first time in the last ten years, I felt like a free man. My faked belief, which I used to declare to my parents, was replaced by a real faith in God. While before I was lying to my family and hid my church attendance from the outside world, now I was truthful to my family and ready to profess my faith without hesitation.

Yes, I was a Christian. No more hiding, no more lying. I told some of my friends – many of them from the army days - of my conversion. They looked at me with some amazement but did not antagonize or judge me. They knew of mad scientists and nutty professors, so maybe I was not an isolated case. Between friends, my madness could be excused and accepted.

As I talked with my colleagues about my faith, there was one, living at our dorm, who showed a high interest. He asked me where I attended church and expressed the desire to read books on the subject. Sure, I could help him. At church. I had access to many books on Christian faith, all of them published in the West and smuggled into the country. I gave him such books, and he told me he read them and asked for more. While I was still happy to help a young man come to Christ, another student told me that my newly-found disciple was a Securitate stooge with the mission to spy on his fellow students. He had been caught by police with some criminal offence and was promised leniency if he collaborated.

***

I started to attend not only the church services, but also the semi-clandestine meetings which took place in the house of Aurel Popescu, the engineer at whose sermon I made the decision to believe in God. He had issued me a blank invitation, followed by specific calls to meetings during the week. The people who attended were Christians of a higher caliber. Many were well-educated, some were professionals, some were poets, composers or writers. Some spent years in prison during the 60s and were closely watched by the Securitate. I found out that many were personal friends of Richard Wurmbrandt, the Jewish Cristian pastor who spent fourteen years in prison and was now living in the West. While the Christians I knew in my hometown of Alba Iulia were from the lower classes and less educated, these people were real intellectuals.

During these meetings, they discussed theology, often with passion. Some knew Ancient Greek and Hebrew and could read the Bible in the original languages. They did not hold to a fixed or uniform theology, which lead to many debates in which theological opinions clashed. Despite this, they were all friends and trusted one another with their lives. As I became more involved, I figured out this loose group was not just about theological debates, but some were involved in clandestine operations like smuggling of Bibles or Christian literature. These activities were secret, and it was no offence to me that for a while I was kept out. If I were a Securitate informer, I could have penetrated the group and passed all acquired knowledge to the police. I am quite sure that some of the participants initially looked at me with some suspicion.

Aurel Popescu was a special man. He had two engineering degrees, worked for a while as a City Hall inspector of state real estate, and preached in various churches all over the country, where he was frequently invited. He was a much sought-after speaker, welcomed in every evangelical church. His sermons were interesting, sometimes funny, and always touched by a special grace. While one may imagine a Baptist preacher under persecution to be a serious man, touched by years of suffering, he was in fact relaxed and happy, with highly contagious *joie de vivre*. He had this gift of speaking in a convincing manner, and we laughed when some official said about him, "When Popescu speaks, it appears it is as he says, but it isn't."

Periodically he had clashes with the Communist authorities. One Sunday, he preached from the text that says, "The fool says in his heart, there is no God." The following Monday, he was called to a Securitate office and an upset officer protested. "Mr. Popescu, here and in the Government, we are all Communists and we do not believe there is a God. Are you calling all of us fools?" Instead of being intimidated, he was amused, and answered with a smile, "Comrade Colonel, you are an Atheist Communist, I am a Christian. We both have strong beliefs. You may believe what you want, and you may quote Marx or Lenin as much as you want. As for me, I am a Christian, I believe in God and I quote the Scripture. As far as I know, so far the Bible is not a forbidden book. If you do not like it, you should forbid it."

***

Aurel Popescu's wife was Valeria, who was a pediatrician, already retired by the time I knew his family.

They had seven children: five daughters and two sons. The oldest daughter was Manuela, who was married and living in Switzerland. Her husband was the grandson of a former Swiss ambassador to Romania who settled in our country at the end of his service. The family was able to regain their Swiss citizenship and emigrate at a time when it was otherwise difficult to leave the country. Manuela went with them.

The second daughter was Marta, married to a quiet and religious man, Mihai. He was somewhat strange and, in time, started to adopt unorthodox theological ideas, including an extreme form of Calvinism, according to which there are two separate human races: those belonging to God and those reserved for eternal punishment. Mihai and Marta had three beautiful children, who often stayed at their maternal grandparents' large apartment. For a while, the family lived in Bucharest, and later moved – of all places – to my home city, Alba Iulia.

The third daughter was Magdalena, married to Tudorel. They lived in Oltenița, a small town south of Bucharest on the Danube river.

The younger children were Andrei – about 17 at the time I met him – and the twins Alex and Lia, who were around fifteen years old.

The fourth daughter was Ana, who was in her third year of engineering school. I met her during one of my first visits and soon started to initiate some conversations with her about one of my favorite writers, Herman Hesse. Later, she told me that she had no interest in the subject, but at the time she was friendly and seemed fascinated in my literary interests. We became friends, and, while we were not officially dating, we continued to meet at church and take long walks together at the end of the services.

In a short time, her father noticed our friendship, and as a good father decided to somehow slow us down. After a church service, he pulled me aside and said,

"Look, Mihai, I have noticed that you and my daughter Ana are good friends. You are a nice guy, I like you, but given the fact that both of you are young and have many years of college ahead of you, I believe it would be better if you slow down a little. Later you and Ana can continue your friendship and see where it leads."

He watched me carefully, then asked, "Do you agree?"

He was able to communicate hard things in a non-threatening and non-offending way. He had the same charm and joie de vivre as always. He seemed more amused than upset. How could I get in an argument with him? I said, "Yes, I understand and agree." Later, he told me that he did not believe me, and he was right, as I continued to meet Ana just like before.

Due to his charm and his way to make the most difficult conversations seem easy, he was often called to intervene in other family situations. Once he was called to talk with one of my friends, who was about to break an engagement with his fiancé'. He told him, "Look young man, this girl is both beautiful and smart. You are neither smart, nor beautiful, so take advantage of your good luck and marry her." They married and had a successful family.

My friendship with Ana continued to grow, and we met more often and took our long walks after church services. Soon, other people at church started to notice, and one time a young

lady pulled me aside and asked in a conspiratorial voice if there was anything going on between Ana and me. I smiled and simply said, maybe. It was fun keeping people guessing.

At the end of my first year in college, I was walking with Ana on a beautiful Sunday evening, when I surprised her: "Would you consider marrying me?" I suppose she did not expect it and did not have any prepared answer, so she said, "I do not believe so. Not at this time." I was a little disappointed, but not too much, as she immediately took and held my hand, and we continued to walk and talk like two people in love. Later, she told me that she went home and told her family what happened over dinner.

"How did you respond?" they asked.

"I said no," she answered.

They all jumped on her: "You made a great mistake. He is a handsome, smart boy and a good Christian. You have made a great mistake."

At the end of the first year of college, I went back to my parents in Alba Iulia. I did not know how I would continue with her, so we did not communicate during the summer. Later, she told me that she waited to hear from me and was sad that I completely disappeared. However, one or two weeks after I returned to Bucharest for my second year, I visited her at home. I was alone with her in the apartment and free to talk.

"Ana," I said, "you know that I proposed to you and you said no. I would like to renew my proposal. Would you marry me?"

This time she said yes. We were engaged, happy, and looking forward to the future. She told her family, who agreed with our plans. I called my parents and surprised them with the announcement, but they were a little upset, not because of who Ana was but because I was young at that time, not yet twenty-two years old. Eventually they agreed, and we were on our way to marriage.

I had to officially ask for Aurel's permission to marry his daughter. He looked at me amused and said,

"Yes, yes, I agree, but you are putting me in a difficult situation. I have a moral dilemma. As Ana's father, I am happy you want to marry her. We like you and we are sure you will be a good husband to her. However, as your brother in Christ I have to say I feel guilty for letting you marry her. You'll have a lot of trouble." Maybe he meant 10% of what he said, but his smile assured me that everything was fine. He always had that sense of humor.

We were married in August of 1977, during the summer vacation between my second and third year of college.

The Objector

I knew that as a practicing and active Christian I would sooner or later run into some trouble with our Communist authorities.

I had already told my close friends of my conversion to Christianity, but I did not make it public at the university. I was by default a member of the Communist Student's Association, as was everybody else. I did not have to sign up for it, so there was no need to explain to anybody that my beliefs were different from those of Communism.

In the second trimester of my first year, the first crack appeared. One afternoon, after we had finished attending a lecture, somebody came and read some names from a list. We were all called to come to a special room, which I knew was used by the local Communist organization of our faculty. As we met there, I realized that they had called only the top students in our year, perhaps about ten of us.

The room had a Communist flag and a big portrait of Ceauşescu on the wall. We were seated at a long table, and soon the secretary of the Communist Faculty organization came in and started to talk to us.

"We called you here for something that may become one of most important events in your lives," he started. "As you can see, you are the top students in your year, and this is not by chance. We know that you will have great careers ahead of you and you can serve your country and the Communist Party with great distinction. As children, you

111

matter, and I knew I would have to make some hard choices.

While few people sincerely agreed with Communism in general and with the Party in particular, the majority of people were keeping their deepest convictions to themselves or discussed them only with their closest friends and family. They signed because they considered it an absurd comedy. You want me to sign? Yes, I will sign, because deep inside I despise the system, and lying on a piece of paper, which is just garbage, means nothing to me. I will sign and move on with my life, because the real life is my circle of friends, my profession, my work, my family, while the official system is just a false reality to which I must pay a tribute. It was just like paying taxes regardless of what you think about how the government is spending the money. Fill the forms, sign, pay, and it's over.

I did not despise these people. I remembered an apparently self-contradicting piece of advice from the book of Proverbs:

Answer not a fool according to his folly, lest thou also be like unto him.

Answer a fool according to his folly, lest he be wise in his own conceit.

(Proverbs 26:4-5 King James Version)

One evening, I was sitting on a bench in a park in my hometown of Alba Iulia, when a man came straight to me, holding (surprise!) a sword in his hand. I had no idea how he got it, as one does not find swords at every corner. He looked quite threatening as he sat next to me and asked me to join him in the fight against evil. I immediately agreed with him and promised to join. He was a fool, a mentally deranged person, and I would have been an even greater fool to start contradicting him. A lot of people treated the Communist Party in the same way. They were fools, and we played the game and agreed with them to avoid their sword.

There is, however, the other case, when one must not answer the fool according to his folly. There was not a clear line between these two instructions, but in this case I decided that I could not go ahead with the game. Like my heroes, Becket and Thomas More and Solzhenitsyn, I had to take a stand, unpleasant as it was. I had no desire to become a hero, and I was rather interested to continue my studies and become a mathematician.

I remembered how, as a thirteen-year-old child, I was terrorized at the thought of my school teachers finding out that I go to church. I remembered how I was a coward when our principal scolded us pupils from Baptist families and I stepped forward and declared that I did not believe in God. At that time, I feared persecution and ridicule. Now I had to redeem myself by taking a stand.

I discussed the dilemma with Ana, and we decided together than neither of us would sign. Interestingly enough, there were many other students in our church in the same situation, but the subject of the loyalty pledge was not discussed among us. I supposed that most of them were afraid and decided to sign, which would have made the subject quite uncomfortable. I kept quiet myself, as I did not want to judge others and I thought it would be disgusting for me to start showing off with a holier-than-thou attitude.

The signing of the pledge was supposed to be a public event. The Party organization was careful to prepare it in advance. As young people are usually idealistic and sometimes revolutionary or rebellious, they did not want any surprises. A commission of professors was formed, and each student had to appear in front of the commission for a brief discussion, which was supposed to flash out any possible opposition. In reality, opposition was not expected, and I heard from other students who had already appeared in front of the commission that the discussion was light and easy. Perhaps most of the members of the commission were rather bored, and the discussions often degenerated in jokes and moved to other subjects like course curriculum or grades.

When my turn came, I entered the room and sat at a table opposite to three or four professors. They knew I was a good student and soon started to ask questions about which direction I intended to take in my studies or which math subjects I was most interested in. The pledge of loyalty to the Communist Party was mentioned only in passing, as if it was an uneventful act of pure administrative importance. They were about to release me when I said, "By the way, I have no intention to sign the pledge." I thought it would be fair to warn them in advance and not make a scene during the signing ceremony.

"What? What do you mean you will not sign?" They were genuinely surprised. I believe most of them liked me, maybe some even sympathized with me, but now they had to do something and they did not know what.

"Why you do not want to sign?"

I had prepared a response which was as tame as possible, carefully avoiding any hint of rebellion or political opposition.

"I was almost ready to sign, but I discovered a problem. While I agree with the Communist Party in many respects, there is a point on which I have different opinions. I am a Christian and I cannot agree with the atheistic philosophy of the Party. That's all."

"So why don't you sign, if you agree with most of the rest?"

"I am ready to sign, provided I can add a note that I do not agree with the atheism promoted by the Party."

"That would not be possible. There is no provision for taking personal exceptions from the content of the pledge."

They let me go but told me that I would be called for further discussions. So far, there were no threats and no imminent danger.

A few days later, I was called again in front of the commission. They were still polite, but this time they put more pressure on me. Having a student refuse to sign the pledge was a bad mark for the Faculty of Mathematics, and they wanted to avoid that. Rather than throwing me to the lions, they wanted to sweep it under the rug and move on. Some of them expressed incredulity at the stupidity of my decision.

"I do not understand you," said one of them. "You are one of our best students, you have a scientific mind and you are capable of sound reasoning. How can you believe in God, especially in our time when science has advanced so much?"

It was hard to respond in a simple way, but I tried.

"I can assure you that I came to believe in God after serious reflection. Yes, I want to be a scientist, I love math and science, but I did not find any contradiction between math and science on one side and belief in God on the other. If you wish, we can discuss the details as much as you'd like. I am prepared."

One of the professors could not let go of his incredulity.

"Tell me," he said, "do you really believe that thunders are provoked by Saint Peter travelling in a carriage through the clouds?"

"No, I do not believe that," I responded, "that is not my faith. In fact, your question makes me believe that you are not really well informed about what the Christian faith is. I can tell you more about my faith, if you wish."

He sighed in desperation. Understanding the Christian faith seemed like a waste of time for him, so he did not pursue it.

It was clear that in this meeting they were only trying to show me the naivety of my position. Perhaps they hoped to lead me step by step to abandon my faith. They were shocked how a rational and intelligent man like me could still believe in God. Soon they gave up but warned me that more would follow.

A few more days passed, and I was called again for a discussion. This time, there was just one man who I did not recognize. He introduced himself as Antonie Iorgovan, the secretary of the Student's Communist Association for all of the University of Bucharest. He was tall and fit, with an aquiline nose and sharp and penetrating eyes.

"Sit down," he said. "I do not have much time for you. What is this stupid refusal to sign the pledge of loyalty for the Party?"

I explained again that I intended no offence and no rebellion, and it was just this little detail about the Party's atheist view which I could not follow.

"Rubbish!" he exclaimed. "Aren't you ashamed of yourself to hold such backward views?"

"As a matter of fact, I am not ashamed," I responded.

"You are a member of the Communist Student's Association, are you not? How did you get there? You are an impostor, claiming to be a Communist while in fact you are a superstitious reactionary."

"I am not a Communist. You know very well that we were all automatically enrolled as we entered college. I had no intention to deceive anybody."

"I will ask you for the last time: are you going to sign?"

"Not if I have to pledge to follow the Communist Party line on atheism."

"OK, then let me tell you what will happen to you. First, you will be excluded from the Communist Student's Association. There will be a public meeting in which your colleagues will expose your stupidity and rebellion and vote to expel you. But that is only act one. Act two, you will be expelled from the University. I will make it my personal goal to throw you out. I can guarantee it will happen."

Now I was cornered. It was no longer a game, and my future was hanging in balance.

"Comrade Iorgovan," I said, "that would be against our state constitution, which guarantees freedom of religion. That includes the right to pursue higher education."

He leaned towards me and said,

"You have no idea. I wrote my PhD thesis on the subject of constitutional law, and I can assure you that the constitution is flexible enough to allow me to throw you out of the University. You will be a nobody. While your colleagues will become scientists or professors, your life will be wasted. You will be thrown in the dustbin of history, where you will soon disappear."

With that he stood up and stormed out of the room.

The big student meeting to exclude me from the Communist Student's Association came a few days later. It was held in a large lecture hall with about 120 students in attendance. Some Party official spoke about the wonderful event coming soon, where everybody would express their love for the Party and gratitude to Comrade Ceaușescu by signing the pledge. Then he mentioned that there is a student who refuses to sign and that this student is not worthy to be part of the Communist Association and should be excluded. He then asked for a vote for my exclusion.

I was sitting in a corner, trying to be as inconspicuous as possible. Some turned and looked at me, some avoided looking, embarrassed by the fact that they would have to vote against a good fellow whom they liked and maybe admired.

"All in favor of exclusion, raise your hand," the man said.

Surprise! Less than half for the students raised their hands.

"All against the exclusion, raise your hand."

More than half raised their hands. This was a major scandal. We lived in an age of unanimity, in which the illusion had to be maintained that any rational person would be loyal to the Communist Party. The system failed.

The leader of the meeting was enraged and started to scold the students. "You proved yourselves without a social and political conscience!" he exclaimed. "This act will have serious consequences, and you who voted against will get in serious trouble." He concluded the meeting in a hurry and left the hall.

Many of the students were genuinely scared. They knew the rules and they knew the dangers. It was clear that the Party would not let this go and there would soon be a second attempt. Some came to me and asked what to do, hoping to hear that I did not care and that I would release them to vote against me, but I did not want to let them off the hook too easily. My answer was, "Vote your conscience. However, if you vote for my exclusion, I will not hold it against you. I will remain your friend and I hope you will remain my friend."

The reality was that I did not care about this "act one," as Antonie Iorgovan called it. I was only afraid of "act two," expulsion from the University. For the moment I even had some fun. One of my colleagues, whom I know from the Army days, came to me and said,

"Do you understand that once you are excluded you lose any chance of becoming a Party member in the future?"

"Yes, I understand," I said, "but this is life, with some good things and some bad things." As if I really cared that I would never be a Communist Party member.

A new commission was formed, and each student in my year had to show up for a discussion. This time there was a single serious question: "Will you vote for Oara's exclusion from the Association? If you don't, you will be in big trouble and your future will be compromised." Each student had to pledge that he or she would vote as the Party wanted.

The second meeting followed after about a week, and this time it went as the organizers wanted. The large majority voted to exclude me. There were one or two exceptions, coming from some close friends. I suppose they announced in advance that in good conscience they could not vote against a good friend, but perhaps they were forgiven, as the main goal of the meeting was achieved anyway.

For the first time in my life, starting from my days as a Communist Pioneer at the age of eight, I was not part of a Communist organization. I felt free and happy. I was no longer involved in the masquerade. I could live in truth. I did not have to say one thing publicly and think the opposite privately.

While I was content with my new situation, I was also worried. The sword of Damocles, hanging on a single hair, was above my head and ready to fall. I remember walking one night through the streets and stopping on a bridge, when I had this frightful vision of a bleak future. I would be expelled from the University. I would not be able to finish college. I would not be able to pursue my passion for mathematics. I would get some humble and boring job somewhere out of Bucharest and I would only work for survival. My parents would be ashamed of me. After such great expectations regarding my future, everything would fall flat. They would have to explain to their friends why I was not able to graduate, and they would feel ashamed. My father would be mad at me for my lack of wisdom.

It was only a temptation of fear and despair. I had to shake off all those thoughts and hope for the best. After all, God was still in control.

***

The "act two" promised by Iorgovan would have fallen on me, except for some other unexpected events at the international and national level.

In July and August of 1975, European leaders organized a conference in Helsinki with the purpose of reducing tensions between the West and the Communist bloc. All European countries participated, with the exception of Albania and Andorra. While no treaty was signed, there was a general accord, which included ten points. The seventh point of the accord expressed the promise of all states "to respect human rights and individual freedom of thought, conscience, religion or belief." This might have been a trap for the Communist countries, which had no intention to abide by this promise, except that their leaders thought that they could manage to suppress any news about violations. Nevertheless, Radio Free Europe informed the citizens of Eastern Europe of the content of the accord, which encouraged many dissidents to accuse their governments of such violations. Many of them wrote letters to foreign leaders and organized movements inside their own countries for the protection of freedom of conscience and religious rights.

A follow-up of the Helsinki conference was scheduled to take place in Belgrade in October of 1977. This generated some degree of unrest in the Communist countries, as dissidents tried to denounce their governments for lack of respect for human rights.

A group of evangelical leaders in the country prepared a document detailing over a hundred cases of religious persecution in Romania. The document, containing open signatures, was secretly sent to the West to be provided to all countries participating at the conference. It was read at Radio Free Europe, so it became public and many Romanian citizens became aware of it. One of the cases of persecution listed in the document was my own. In a few lines, it related the story of the loyalty oath imposed on Romanian citizens and the threats made against me, including the threat to be expelled from university. I believe this is what saved my education, as the authorities did not want to give further ammunition to any foreign observer following up on the cases.

The signatories of the document were taking a great personal risk. One of them was my future father-in-law, Aurel Popescu. There were two other prominent Baptist pastors, Iosif Ton and Pavel Niculescu. There was also a Pentecostal, a Brethren, and possibly an Adventist.

The morning after the document was read at Radio Free Europe, the Securitate agents showed up at the house of my father-in-law and picked him up. He was taken to their famous building on Calea Rahovei Street, where a major investigation was started, perhaps at the order of Ceaușescu himself. The purpose of the investigation was to find out how the document was sent outside of the country and possibly to indict the signatories. The investigation lasted for six weeks.

My father-in-law was not arrested, but he had the obligation to show up at the Securitate building every morning, where he was interrogated for hours. He was not beaten or tortured, and he told us that he was struck on the face only once, by a frustrated officer. He never lost his sense of humor. Every evening we gathered at his house where he related the events of that day. He was a good story teller and we often laughed as he repeated the conversations he had. One such conversation I remember.

Towards the end of the investigation, a colonel came to the interrogation room and told him:

"Mister Popescu, we are about to close our investigation. Personally, I would like to let you go, but we have orders to indict you. This gives me a problem, for I am not sure of what to accuse you. I have looked through our Penal Code and the only crime that fits your case is treason."

"I appreciate your problem, Colonel," my father-in-law responded. "I would like to ask you what the punishment is if I am found guilty?"

"Very simple, it is life in prison or the death penalty."

"That is very serious. Could you not find something lighter, something that would be punished with just a few years in prison?"

"With all my regret, I could not find anything else. That is a pity, as I really like you and we became quite good friends in the last weeks."

After a few moments in which the gravity of the situation was supposed to sink into him, my father-in-law came up with an idea.

"Comrade Colonel, I think I can help you find something better. Can you provide me with a copy of the Penal Code?"

"Sure, it's right here." He handed my father-in-law a book he picked from a shelf.

My father-in-law took the book and started to browse it, stopping at some promising paragraphs. Then he turned to the colonel and said,

"As I can see, there are many alternatives: denigration of the Socialist order, insult to the authorities, even spreading false rumors. Of course, this is not the case here, but I would rather have you falsely accuse me of some crime then of treason, which may result in the death penalty."

"We'll see," responded the colonel, amused.

Some of the other co-conspirators followed other trajectories through the investigation. Pavel Niculescu, who was recalcitrant and noisy, was actually beaten. His strategy was to shout with all his voice, "They beat me! They beat me! Stop hitting me!" with the hope to scare the officers. It may have worked to a certain degree.

Josef Ton followed another method. He was a man educated at Oxford and tried to pass as a statesman willing to find a compromise between the Communist authorities and the Christians. He suggested a small change in the Communist ideology, the abandonment of atheism, while preserving all the lofty socialist ideals. He tried to convince them that this would result in international admiration and a real revival of the people's love for Communism. Unfortunately, it was a quixotic attempt, and he was never taken seriously.

The investigation was closed, and nobody was indicted. The Securitate could not convince any of the signatories to retract or give actionable information about how they communicated with Radio Free Europe.

***

1977 was a year of many earthquakes. One of these was literal

On March 4, 1977, I was with Ana at her family's apartment, along with some of her brothers and several visitors. At 9:22 PM, I felt a minor vibration, which I thought it was some large truck going down the boulevard in front of our building. After a few seconds, the vibration intensified, and we heard a rumbling that seemed to come from deep inside the earth. The house started to shake and some windows broke. At that moment, we knew it was an earthquake. We heard explosions and the lights went out. We tried to run outside, but it was impossible to walk, as the floor was dancing under our feet. The earthquake lasted for 56 seconds, and we found out later that it was 7.2 on the Richter scale.

When it ended, we all ran outside. We looked at our building: a big crack ran from the first floor to the fourth floor, traversing the outside wall of the living room where we were during the earthquake. If the shaking continued a few more seconds, the building would have collapsed. I could see my parents mourning for their son who died at the age of twenty-two.

The street was full of people who ran out of the buildings. As we thought it unsafe to go back inside, Ana and I decided to take a walk towards the center. We crossed Union Plaza and headed towards Nicolae Bălcescu Boulevard. Ambulances and fire trucks were racing in all directions, while rivers of people were walking up and down the boulevard. After we passed the Intercontinental Hotel, we came to a nightmare scene. A few ten-story buildings had collapsed, and now they were just huge piles of rubble under which hundreds of human bodies were buried. One of the piles was where the Scala Building had been standing before. We found out later that two of our friends were crushed there as they were enjoying a coffee in one of the restaurants.

When the earthquake happened, Ceauşescu was in an African country for a state visit. He interrupted the visit and came home the next morning to take charge of the situation. The Party newspapers used the situation for more propaganda, which few people believed. About two weeks after the earthquake, the official Party newspaper *Scânteia* (The Spark) ran a story which related how Elena Ceauşescu visited one of the sites where workers were still removing rubble. The workers told her that by that time it was impossible to find survivors. However, animated by her high humanism and enlighten by her wisdom, she said, "No, there are more survivors. Dig here!" The workers obeyed her, and, low and behold, they found an eighteen-year-old boy alive in the ruins.

Later, the rumor was that this was in fact a gypsy boy on a looting expedition, who just happened to be there.

***

Another active dissident at that time was the Romanian writer Paul Goma, who was harassed by the Securitate for having written an open letter – read at Radio Free Europe – in which he criticized the Communist regime. He had a long history of opposition to the Communist Party.

In 1956, he had attempted to organize a student strike, was arrested, and spent two years in prison. After he was released, he spent many more years under house arrest and then as a simple manual laborer, not being allowed to enter the university again. Only in 1965 was he able to continue his studies at the Faculty of Letters of the University of Bucharest. In 1968, in appreciation of Ceauşescu's condemnation of the invasion of Czechoslovakia by Warsaw Pact countries, he requested and was admitted as a member of the Communist Party. The honeymoon did not last too long. He wrote a novel, *Ostinato*, based on his experiences with the secret police, which was not published in Romania, having been rejected by the censorship. They discovered that one of the characters bore a close resemblance to Elena Ceauşescu, the dictator's wife.

Now, in 1977, he wrote a public letter expressing solidarity with the Charter 77 movement in Czechoslovakia, which criticized the Communist regime. Some of his friends and associates signed the letter with him, but before more people got the chance to sign, the Securitate intervened and started to harass him. His apartment was constantly watched and the Securitate agents did not allow other people to visit him and sign.

Paul Goma was the child who cried "the Emperor has no clothes!" He treated his Securitate interrogators or tormentors as dimwitted street muggers and refused to live in fear. At a certain point, he wrote a second public letter to president Ceauşescu, asking him to co-sign the initial letter, since they – Ceauşescu and Goma – were the only ones who did not fear the Securitate.

One day, a group of Securitate agents arrived at his apartment, where he was living with his wife Ana Maria, to arrest him. Here is a fragment in which he tells the story of his arrest. (I translated and slightly adapted it for an American audience.)

> *At Hristenco's signal they start pushing the door to get inside.*

> *"Why do you push? Why do you push?" I cry, and I push them back. Losing balance, two of them fall over some bottles stacked near the door.*

> *Hristenco closed the door from inside. He says, breathing heavily:*

> *"Do not let yourselves be provoked. Let us not be provoked!" Together with two others, they immobilize me between their bellies.*

"Anaaa!" I cry from their claws, "they came to arrest me!"

Comrade Hristenco tries to put his hand on my mouth, but misses it. I am pushed into the living room. Ana Maria comes from the child's room. She seems surprised. She asks:

"Do you have a warrant for his arrest? If not – out!"

"We do," says Hristenco, happy that this question came, and not another, and he pulls a paper from his briefcase.

I take it... but it's impossible! On the bed, on my bed, sit two women: the building superintendent and another old woman from the first floor. When and how did they get here? I postpone the answer. I read aloud the paper from Hristenco. It is an arrest warrant indeed.

"The reasons, the accusations," demands Ana Maria.

"In accordance with the article..." I read. What? "Treason?"

"You are traitors, not him," shouts Ana Maria to the Securitate agents.

"Don't let yourselves be provoked, comrades," says Hristenco to his people, *and he tries to pick the paper from my hands.*

"I am the accused, I have the right to know what the accusation is!"

"You will find out when we get there… you will find out after…"

"After what? When?" jumps Ana Maria. "Where? First you arrest him, then you tell him the reason? Read further," she orders me.

"Second reason. Wow! Relations against nature! What are 'relations against nature'?"

"Everything will be explained there," says Hristenco, trying to take the paper from my hand.

I do not have to play some game with Ana Maria, she knows my talents and defects, but now I have other witnesses, the two women.

"'Relations against nature,' that is homosexuality. Pederasty. Bravo! Could you not find anything else? Treason against the country and pederasty! Let's say I betrayed

*my country, but pederasty? What did I do,
have sex with Ceaușescu?"* (my note: Goma
was using much stronger words, including
references to anatomical parts.)

*A shout of terror from the Securitate
agents. No one had ever heard such
blasphemy before.*

*"Let us not be provoked, comrades, let
us not," continues to shout Hristenco, trying
to cover my voice in case I utter another
blasphemy. Now he succeeds in pulling the
paper from my hands.*

While this fragment was read at Radio Free Europe
much later, during those fateful months in 1977, in the
evenings our ears were glued to the radios, awaiting news
about the dissidents from Radio Free Europe. Most people
sympathized with those brave individuals who dared to
speak but were still too afraid to follow their example.

***

Ana graduated with an engineering degree in 1978,
while I was still a student. According to the common
practice, she appeared in front of a job placement
commission where she had to choose between a number of
listed positions, all of them outside Bucharest. She picked a
job in the city of Deva, not far from Alba Iulia where my
parents lived, and we had to go through a temporary forced
separation.

Her job was completely inappropriate for a young married lady. She was supposed to work on a construction site with tough and rugged workers, at a place where they did not even have a ladies' room. She stayed with a Baptist family, as her father was popular, and many offered to provide her with a room. To overcome these unpleasant circumstances, we had a plan which in the end worked quite well. We waited a few months, then her father went into action. Although he was already fired from his powerful job at Bucharest City Hall, he still had plenty of friends there. He talked with one of these friends, who made a special request to hire her in a position with a state enterprise (known for its initials as ICRAL) responsible for building maintenance all over the city. Soon she was back in Bucharest with me, and we lived in a small apartment at a far edge of the city. Later, we moved in her nice family apartment in the center.

I remember two incidents she had in her job, indicative of her personality and of the general atmosphere and culture in the country.

One of her colleagues, another engineer, was spending all day chain smoking in a corner of the building where they worked. Nobody bothered him, and all others joked and laughed when they saw him doing nothing.

"How come you never work?" Ana asked him jokingly at one time when she passed him.

"These people are not worth my effort," he answered, puffing from his cigarette.

In this case, "these people" were not his colleagues, nor his immediate bosses, but the whole system, starting with Nicolae Ceaușescu and his wife, Elena, who was praised in newspapers and on TV as a great scientist. After reading in the newspapers about her international prestige of and about the happiness of the Romanian people, very few took the system seriously. There was a common saying, not only in Romania but also in other Communist countries: "We make believe we work, they make believe they pay." There was a general atmosphere of apathy, a conviction that hard work did not improve someone's status in life. Improvements came from pulling social and political strings through chains of personal connections, through little operations on the black market, or through an underground economy more or less tolerated by the state. The only exceptions were the consummate professionals who found meaning in their narrow domain or Party activists who struggled to be promoted to higher positions.

Ana was pregnant while she worked at ICRAL and she made sure not to exert herself too hard. Once, all employees were asked in a meeting to come and work on a Sunday. This was a common occurrence. Work on Sunday was a signal from the local bosses to their higher-ups that they are mobilizing the people to fulfill the economic objectives set by the Party. In most cases, it was unnecessary. Better results could have been achieved by incenting the workers, but that was out of fashion and did not earn points for the class of managers and local Party leaders. They had to report that people made the extra effort not because they were promised something, but due to their enthusiastic love for the country and the Party.

The director announced: "This Sunday I want to see everybody at the office at nine in the morning. I will go through all the offices and personally note if somebody is missing."

Ana raised her hand, and said, "I will not come to work this Sunday."

"How dare you defy my order?" the director asked with incredulity in his voice. "Do you realize you'll be in trouble?"

"I am pregnant and I need my rest," Ana replied.

"So what? Sitting at your desk does not do you any harm."

"Comrade director," Ana responded, "I want to have a healthy baby. I do not want to give birth to a handicapped child."

At that point, the director's anger suddenly melted, and he moved on to another subject. Ana was initially intrigued by his sudden withdrawal, but later found out that he had a handicapped child. Unknowingly, she had touched a sensitive chord. Later, her colleagues came and praised her for her stand. Even when silent, the great majority appreciated when somebody defied authority.

The Underground Activist

In 1977, that fateful year of the great earthquakes, I began to be more and more involved in various underground activities. I cannot call them illegal, as theoretically there were no laws against most of them. When, in 1956, Goma organized a student strike, he was not breaking any law. According to the official propaganda, we were supposed to be a free people, free to associate, to organize strikes, to express any political opinions, or to build churches. However, if one engaged in some of these activities, the Securitate intervened and the "free" person often ended up in prison.

A good example of free but not really free involved our meetings with foreign citizens. There was no law against it and the official media never mentioned it as something illegal. However, in most articles or stories, a meeting with a foreigner was presented as dangerous, often resulting in some form of corruption and ultimately treason. In schools, the teachers advised us to avoid meeting foreigners, implying that it might have been illegal. If by chance some German tourist stopped to ask for directions, one was advised to immediately report it to the police. If a longer discussion occurred, a log must be written.

As Baptists, we received many Western visitors, sometimes from the UK but mostly from the United States. Almost every month, some pastor from Texas or California arrived in Bucharest on a "mission" trip. Most of them called themselves missionaries, as their trips were considered mission trips by their churches. They reported

138

home about what they saw, about some of our problems and needs, and occasionally sent us money or books. Such visits were beneficial for us, as they increased our visibility in the West, which implicitly gave us some protection from arbitrary acts of religious persecution. I was one of the few people in my church who spoke good English, and as such, I was often asked to interpret. I helped our people talk to American visitors, which put me close to the center of the action. Eventually, I came to serve as interpreter for visitors who preached in our church.

Interpreting a sermon was a challenge. I had to not only translate accurately, but also follow the emotional nuances of the English speaker. When he raised his voice, I raised my voice. When he whispered, I whispered. Some preachers wend for long phrases without a break, which forced me to carefully memorize long passages to render them in Romanian without missing everything. Other speakers broke the sentences in the middle to allow me to translate, which occasionally created a problem, as the order of words and grammatical structures were different between the two languages. In such cases, I made a sign to the speaker to complete the phrase, so I could understand what he meant.

Somehow, I became the most popular interpreter of English "missionaries" in Bucharest, while other large cities had other talented interpreters. Some were good, some made occasional blunders.

Once, in the western city of Timisoara, an American preacher wanted to illustrate the beauty of loyalty by using some cute story.

He started: "Once, I came to visit one of my friends. I rang the bell, and he opened the door. Next to him was a German Shepherd."

The interpreter had a limited understanding of the English language and American culture, and he thought that "German Shepherd" was a German pastor, as "shepherd" and "pastor" are occasionally synonyms in Romanian (as they may also be in English), so he translated:

"Once, I came to visit one of my friends. I rang the bell, and he opened the door. Next to him was a pastor from Germany."

Then, the preacher continued: "The German Shepherd came next to me and started to lick my hand."

The Romanian interpreter stopped for a moment, sensing that something was wrong, but tried to make a slight correction, translating this as "The German pastor came next to me and started to kiss me."

It got worse from there. The preacher said, "Then he jumped on me."

The interpreter said, "He came and embraced me."

The preacher said: "He was waging his tail."

At that point, the interpreter was lost. Some people in the audience who understood English started to laugh." Neither the preacher nor the interpreter understood what was going on. They interrupted the normal course of the story and started a private conversation. Eventually, the Romanian interpreter, with a red face, said, "I apologize, it was not a German pastor, but a dog of the breed German Shepard."

Although I had my set of blunders, they were never quite so bad.

The American "missionaries" were not of high interest for the Securitate. I believe the Communist authorities allowed them to come, hoping to create the impression that the Baptists were free to live and function in Romania.

We had, however, other kinds of visitors. Some were political figures from the United States or the U.K. Once, we hosted a group of Conservative MPs from UK, who came to my father-in-law's apartment and discussed the issue of religious freedom in Communist Romania. We fully briefed them on all forms of obstruction and persecution happening in the country. This was more dangerous and could have landed us in prison if the authorities knew what was being discussed.

There was an even more dangerous category: that of Westerners who came for super-secret work. Some were involved with smuggling operations. They organized illegal transports of Bibles or religious literature. Some came to secretly support persecuted Christians with money for churches or for the families of people in prison. There was an organization in UK for the study of religion and Communism, and their people came to find out what was happening in our country.

We met all these people and worked with them. We had no idea how much the Securitate knew, and we had no intention to help them know more.

There was one American visitor - I will call him Peter- with whom I spent many hours and who I took to various locations to meet people. He taught me some rudimentary techniques of what one may call spycraft. No, we were not spies, we did not work for a foreign government and we were not betraying our country. However, some security measures were both useful and necessary. One of the techniques he taught me was how to spot surveillance.

"When you walk on the street in the city, do not look back. That may alert your pursuers, if any. Rather, when you take a corner, always use the side of the sidewalk close to the street, not the one close to the building. That way, you can throw a glance back in a natural manner. Try to notice if there are any suspicious characters, or at least to memorize some of the faces of the people coming behind you. Then, after a few blocks, take another turn and use the same technique, trying to figure if you see the same faces as before."

Another technique: "Even if you do not know if you are being followed, you can ensure nobody is after you by changing buses often. Jump into the bus at the last moment before the door closes, but in a natural way, as if you just made your mind to take that bus. See if anybody else tries to do the same, or if anyone comes running after the bus."

Soon, I was about to start using these pieces of advice.

***

The threat of being expelled from the University was still hanging over my head. The sword could fall at any time, shattering my dreams of becoming a professional mathematician.

One day, I was descending the steps of the main stairs of the Faculty of Mathematics, when my philosophy teacher stopped and dragged me to a corner. His name was Vasile Tonoiu, and I believe his title was that of a lecturer. He had studied philosophy at the Sorbonne, in France, and he looked like what I believe would be a typical French philosopher of the late 60's, with long hair, thin, and animated by an inexhaustible energy. I knew something else about him: although he was not a declared Christian, he was the son of a known Christian leader who knew my father-in-law.

"Look, Oara," he said, "I have something important to tell you. I was asked to fail you at the philosophy exam." He looked intensely at me to see how I would react. I kept my cool.

"However," he continued, "I will not do that. But I cannot give you the maximum grade which you will perhaps deserve, as that would get me into a lot of trouble. So, instead of getting a 10 (the equivalent of an A), I will give you a lower grade, maybe an 8 (the equivalent of a B- or a C). Do you have any problem with that?"

"No, I don't," I answered. "I completely understand your situation. I am not upset at all. In fact, I would like to thank you for giving me some protection. I was once threatened to be expelled, so this is not too bad."

The following week, during the examination, I did quite well. Any other student would have gotten the maximum grade, but I got an 8, as he promised. That spoiled my record, as before I had the maximum grade for all subjects, but that was a small price to pay compared to possible expulsion.

However, I had my revenge. In the days before the exam, I had received a few packages with books. They were all copies of *Marx and Satan*, written by Richard Wurmbrandt. Both the title and the author could have sent me directly to prison. Richard Wurmbrandt had been a political prisoner for fourteen years in Romania and was now in the West, speaking in front of the US Congress about religious persecution in Romania. He was considered an enemy of the people by the authorities, who let him go out of the country only at the intervention of some influential Western politicians.

The book was well documented and attempted to show that Marx was a Satanist. As an example, he showed some of the verses that Marx wrote in his youth:

Then I will be able to walk triumphantly,
Like a god, through the ruins of their kingdom.
Every word of mine is fire and action.
My breast is equal to that of the Creator.

And another one:

See this sword?
the prince of darkness
Sold it to me.

While Communism claimed to bring happiness to mankind, the book showed that its number one father, Karl Marx, was a hater of mankind, a destroyer, a disciple of Satan. It was by far the most dangerous book, which I not only possessed but helped distribute. From all my secret activities, this would have surely landed me in prison.

The day of the philosophy examination, I was supposed to give a number of copies to one of my contacts who was travelling to Moldova. I stuffed my briefcase with as many as I could and went to the University. During the examination, I placed the briefcase next to my feet, and I had a feeling of exaltation. After Vasile Tonoiu handed me the artificially lowered grade, I picked up the briefcase and walked out of the examination room with a big smile on my face.

You fools! I thought. *You try to undermine me by unrighteous means, yet I subvert you by righteous means.*

I went to Gara de Nord, the main rail station in Bucharest, met my contact, and handed him the books.

***

Marx and Satan was not the only book I was secretly receiving and distributing. I was not so much involved with Bibles as with other kinds of Christian literature. Bibles were handled by other networks, of which I did not know too much and did not want to know more. In this type of work, compartmentalization was important, which meant not only to not pass information to those who are not needed to act on it, but also not to find by chance information which was not important for your work. If I

145

were interrogated, I would have divulged no secrets about Bible smuggling, not because I was strong, but because I knew nothing or very little.

I do not know who translated and published Christian books in Romanian. I suppose initially there were Romanian Baptist churches in America, but eventually other organizations got involved. We had a constant supply coming in.

One afternoon, an Englishman arrived at my apartment and told me that he had a small transport of Christian books in Romanian. I had never met him before. Today, people would have papers and invoices and letters. They would have long meetings and discussions. At that time, everything had to be short and efficient. No papers exchanged, no signatures.

The Englishman was around thirty-five years old. He told me that his wife and baby were in a car parked two blocks from my apartment. I suggested we take turns going between the car and the apartment and to carry one handbag with books at a time, as to not raise suspicions. He described to me his car and told me to go first. There was, though, an aspect which we forgot. His wife did not know me and did not know that a young man was coming to pick up books. When I arrived at her car and opened the door, she thought I might be a thief, a scary prospect for a young woman in a foreign country with a baby in the car. She was terrified and started to shout at me to get out, which I promptly did. I went back to the apartment and told her husband what had just happened. Now he went first and explained to his wife the mechanics of the operation. After that, things went as planned.

***

After a Sunday evening service, our pastor, Vasile Taloş, called me and another young man and told us that he wanted us to work with some people from the West who were running a discipleship ministry. I would soon find out that these were the Navigators, an organization started by a fellow called Dawson Trotman sometime in the 1930s. Among other things, the Navigators taught young people how to memorize Scripture and how to practice personal evangelism. They had a structured program with careful and personal attention to everyone involved. Once a disciple went through all the steps, he was supposed to gather other disciples and continue to multiply the ministry, depending on his level of skill, maturity and dedication.

We had many meetings in various homes in Bucharest, including at my apartment. The meetings were always held in maximum secrecy. We arrived at the meeting place at different times and never left together. We made sure not to be too noisy, so as not to attract the attention of the neighbors.

There was an all-country leadership in which I was included. Once a year, the leadership met and held strategy sessions and advanced courses.

One year we met in the city of Cluj, in Transylvania, which was about seventy miles from my home city of Alba Iulia. We organized a secret camp in the forest and stayed there for a whole week. During this time, we had a bizarre encounter which now seems a little humorous, but at that time created some serious apprehension.

We were enjoying our time around a camp fire when we heard some noise not too far. As we looked, we noticed a man looking at us from distance of about fifty yards. Even if he was not a policeman, he could have been an informer or even an innocent who later would go back to the city and talk about what he had seen. We had to find out what his business was. Two of us, myself and a tall and handsome guy called Philip, went to talk to him.

"Good evening, what are you doing here?" Philip asked.

The man looked at us with some suspicion and seemed unsure of himself.

"Good evening," he answered. "I am just wandering around."

"Nice evening isn't it?" asked Philip.

"It's certainly a nice evening," he responded.

We were all a little embarrassed and perhaps a little afraid.

"You must have some business here," tried Philip. "We are having a summer camp. Would you like to eat something with us?"

"No, no… no big deal, I was only…" Now he seemed frightened.

"Hey, we do not care what you are doing."

148

Now he confessed: "I was gathering some wood. Please do not tell anybody. It's just a few pieces, it won't hurt anybody."

Now we understood. The man was illegally gathering wood from the forest and was scared that somebody would turn him in to the authorities. We were engaged in different kinds of illegal activities.

"Don't worry," Philip calmed him. "We do not care. You surely need it for your family, perfectly understood. At the same time, it would be a good idea not to tell anybody about our camp. Who knows, maybe other people will think to come and enjoy this spot, and suddenly we would have a lot of people around, and that would not be fun."

"Certainly, certainly," the man said and disappeared into the forest, happy for not being caught.

***

During the investigation of the six Christians who signed the letter to the Belgrade Conference, my father-in-law was told in no uncertain terms that it would be a good idea for him to leave the country. It was an offer hard to refuse. He thought it over and discussed the subject with his family and friends. There were many reasons not to leave. He was around sixty at that time, not a good age to start a new life. He was a great force among Evangelical Christians and his presence would have been greatly missed. On the other hand, he had reasons to leave. By now, the Securitate was watching him closely, which prevented him from being engaged in some activities that required a degree of secrecy. Not only was he in danger, but he was endangering other people who he met. Then there was the issue of his three younger children, who he wanted to save from future trouble. In the end, he decided to emigrate to the United States.

Getting a passport to leave Romania was very difficult. Some people applied for a passport to emigrate, but then were fired from their jobs and had to wait years after years without getting the much-desired passport. Some people tried to cross the border illegally, at a great risk to their lives. One could be shot, or caught, beaten, and thrown into prison. Some went through all this Calvary, then tried again. Perhaps the safest way to leave was by not returning after a tourist trip. There were problems with that too: it was difficult to get a tourist passport to visit the West. An easier solution was to travel to Yugoslavia (where travel was approved much easier than the West) and then try to illegally cross into Italy. The Yugoslav police did not shoot people. If one was caught, his fate was like a toss of the coin: some were allowed to continue to Italy, some were arrested and returned to Romanian authorities. Some people were lucky to be allowed to travel to the West for professional reasons, and of these, some defected and never returned. We even had a joke about this. Question: "What is the definition of a quartet?" Answer: "A Romanian symphonic orchestra returning from a tour in the West."

The family of my father-in-law did not have to go through any of these risky scenarios. He applied to leave with his younger children and was approved and had all the passports in less than three months. After all, the authorities wanted him to leave the country.

***

Through my father-in-law, I had the opportunity to meet Father Gheorghe Calciu, a truly remarkable person. In normal times, we Evangelicals did not cooperate with the Orthodox, but this was not a normal time.

Gheorghe Calciu had gone through one of the most horrifying experiences in Communism: the so-called Piteşti Experiment. (Piteşti is a city in Romania, where the prison in which the experiment took place was located.) The Experiment was a new method of reeducation of political prisoners, invented by some sick mind. The torturers noticed that when a prisoner was tortured, he could recover after some time of rest alone in his cell or after the encouragement offered to him by his cell mates. The idea was to make torture a twenty-four-hour activity, carried out not by the prison staff but by other inmates.

The authors of this new method took an initial set of prisoners – most of them students accused of having been part of the fascist organization The Iron Guard – and tortured them to the point where they became completely malleable. In the next step, they placed all of them in a cell in which they later brought in another unsuspecting inmate. The "reeducated" inmates were initially friendly with him, but at a predetermined signal, they jumped on him and started to beat him. The beating continued day and night, until the newcomer was completely broken and ready to be reused in the reeducation process. When a complete set of reeducated prisoners was ready, they were placed in a new cell and the process was repeated. The victims had no respite, no time to recover their strength, no friends to console them.

The Experiment was initially "successful," producing more and more broken people and some deaths in the

151

process. However, after a while, the news about what was happening started to trickle through various prisons, then out of the prison system, and eventually to the West. At that point, the authorities panicked, decided to stop it and blame some of the prisoners for what had happened. A trial was arranged, and – after careful preparation – they all admitted their guilt, and were sentenced to death and shot. Except one: Gheorghe Calciu, who during the trial denied his guilt.

I did not know all this at the time when I met Father Calciu, but I read about it shortly thereafter.

In 1964, there was a general amnesty of political prisoners, and he was let out of prison. He completed his education, studied theology, and eventually became priest at a church in Bucharest.

In 1977, he started to preach a series of sermons which attracted a large number of people, the majority of which were students. He did not criticize the regime directly, but his sermons encouraged people to stand for their faith and not let fear take over their lives. More and more people – in the thousands – came to his church, and the authorities were alarmed and started to watch him closely and put pressure on him to stop.

Father Calciu is one of the most remarkable people I have met in my life. He was short, with rapidly graying hair and the goatee which many Orthodox priests favored. He was like a diamond sculptured by the vicissitudes of life, but at the same time exuded love and wisdom. He was the best illustration of what I knew "meek" to mean: confidence and power under perfect control. He had large and generous opinions of all Christians, who he treated with respect, regardless of if they were Orthodox or not. He was eager to collaborate with us. The Orthodox did not have the same extensive connections in the West as we Evangelicals had, so we could help him by making his activities known outside the country. We could also use various channels to send his sermons or writings to the West, where they could be read at Radio Free Europe. In time, we could offer some other help in the form of support for his family when he was eventually arrested again and sentenced to another ten years in prison.

***

Ana and I, along with many other Christians, relatives, and acquaintances, went to the Otopeni airport to see my in-laws leave. It was an emotional event and I saw many people crying. They flew first to Rome, where they stayed in a refugee camp for about a month, and then went to the United States and settled in Oregon, where former friends prepared accommodations for them.

Ana and I came back to our home, which was strangely quiet after the frantic activities of the previous days. We inherited from them an apartment a little too large by common Romanian standards, with four bedrooms, a kitchen, a bathroom, and a supersized living room. Even better, the apartment was in an elegant villa in walking distance to the city center. How could a Christian dissident have such a nice apartment? The explanation was that my father-in-law, before being fired, worked for many years as an inspector in the City of Bucharest department which controlled all state real estate in the city. He had waited for a good apartment to become available, and when one appeared, he rented it for his family. The people who had to approve the lease were his friends. Now it was all ours, which seemed to be a blessing, except that in the end it gave us a lot of trouble.

Our home soon became a hotbed of conspiratorial activities. Most secret activities in which my father-in-law was involved now fell on my shoulders, as he left me as his replacement. Sometimes, late in the evening, the bell would ring and an American would show up to tell me he had a bunch of smuggled books to unload. Many times, I organized Navigator meetings at our place.

One of the most dangerous but also funny secret activities was to distribute funds received from the West. In most cases, the money was for Christians under severe persecution, such as when a man was fired and could not support his family, or a church had to quickly finish the construction of an extension before the authorities noticed. Sometimes, the money was for political figures.

Some American or Englishman I did not know would simply show up at my apartment, and, after he made sure who I was, would hand me the money in Romanian currency, lei. Although the official exchange rate at that time was 12 lei for a dollar, in terms of purchasing parity one leu could generally buy in Romania as much as dollar could buy in the United States. I received large amounts, 5,000 lei, 10,000 lei, or 30,000 lei, with a list of contacts to distribute among. While I always discharged this duty with utmost correctness, I also had some strange encounters.

I took a bus to a remote place at the periphery of Bucharest and struggled to find some obscure apartment in a large block of flats placed among other many buildings. I had to find a person, let's say Maria Ionescu, at apartment 12B. I rang the bell and waited. A plump middle-aged lady came to the door.

"Excuse me," I said, "are you Mrs. Maria Ionescu?"

"Yes," she said, surprised to see a stranger at her door.

"Ma'am, I am supposed to deliver to you this package." I handed her a bunch of one hundred lei bills, wrapped in a paper.

She unwrapped it, looked at me, then looked at the money again.

"I have to leave," I said. "Goodbye."

I turned and left without any other explanation. I did not know who she was, and she did not know who I was. It looked like a theater of the absurd authored by the Romanian dramatist Eugen Ionescu.

Once, I discovered that one of the names on the list was a gentleman named Brătianu, a name well known in Romania. The Brătianu family was active in Romanian politics from the second part of the XIX century, and gave the country many statesmen, including prime ministers. One of the Brătianus was at the head of the Liberal party, which lost the elections to Communists in the late 1940s through electoral fraud. Later, he was arrested and thrown into prison, where he died many years later, after a long suffering and forgotten by the world. During Communism, the name Brătianu was synonymous with enemy of the people. The Brătianu to whom I was to deliver the money was without doubt a descendent of the great family, maybe even the son of the one imprisoned and killed by the Communists. In the eyes of the authorities, helping him was like helping Hitler.

To my surprise, he lived in an apartment less than five minutes from mine. I went there eager to meet a real Brătianu. I carefully scanned the sidewalk in front of the building to see if there was any surveillance. When I rang the bell, an old and frail man came out.

"Mister Brătianu?" I asked.

"Yes," he responded, hesitantly.

I felt free to talk, as there was nobody on the stairs.

"Sir, I am supposed to deliver this to you." I took the package from my trench coat.

He did not take it, but looked at me with sadness in his eyes.

"Who are you?" he asked.

"My name does not matter," I answered. "I have a limited role, just to give you this money, and I will be on my way."

"Are you with the Securitate?"

"No." Unfortunately it was impossible to prove it. "I am honored to meet you, and I am humbly asking you to take it."

He thought for a few seconds, then said, "Young man, you may be honest, but I do not know who you are. This could be a provocation from the Securitate. I am very sorry, I cannot accept the money."

"I am very sorry too, but I will leave and not bother you anymore."

There was nothing else I could do. If I continued to insist, I would have only made him more suspicious. I said goodbye and left with a heavy heart. When the foreign citizen who brought the money arrived again, I explained the situation and was prepared to hand back the money. Instead, he asked me to use it for any other worthy causes of my choice.

***

In April of 1978, the Navigators organized an important meeting with the leaders all over the country, in the city of Arad, close to the border with Hungary. My plan was this: On Friday, I would travel to the meeting by car with one of the American Navigators who happened to be in Bucharest. I would be in the meeting on Saturday and Sunday, and then, although the conference was to continue for another day, fly home Monday morning to take an exam. The plan worked out fine for the first three days, but then I ran into trouble.

The meeting was at the house of one of the members of the leadership, Ovidiu, a good friend of mine. On Saturday, at the end of the meeting, Ovidiu arranged for somebody, who I really did not know, to pick me up and take me to his apartment. We took trams and buses and arrived at a typical area with blocks of flats. I did not know, and indeed I did not want to know, the exact address of the apartment. I stayed there overnight.

The following day, on Sunday, at the end of the meeting, Ovidiu and his wife Ligia asked me to stay and sleep at their house. In the morning, I woke up early and took a bus to the airport in Timişoara, a large city very closet o Arad, where I had spent the night.

In those days, security at the airport was not as strict or sophisticated as it is today, so I did not expect any trouble. There were occasionally some random checks of a traveler's luggage, but I was still not too troubled when a policeman asked me to open my briefcase. After all, I did not have any incriminating documents with me. The policeman looked inside and picked up my Bible, which was not in any way something illegal. He asked me, "Whose is this?" and I responded calmly, "It is mine."

He took it away and asked me to take a seat and wait for somebody to talk to me. My only worry at that point was that I might miss my flight, as on the same day I had to show up for the exam.

A man in uniform came, introduced himself as a police captain, and invited me into his office. After he checked my identification papers, he opened the Bible and looked at the first page, which had some handwritten notation.

"I see here the name Valeria Popescu," he said. "Who is she?"

"She is my mother-in-law," I responded. Indeed, she left me her Bible when she departed for America.

"Where is she now?"

"She is in the United States. She emigrated there with the rest of her family."

"By the way," I continued, "as far as I know, it is not a crime to have a Bible, so I really do not know why you stopped me. My flight leaves in forty-five minutes. I have to make sure I catch it."

"We decide when you go," he retorted sharply. "First, you have to answer some questions."

"Sure, I will answer any question you ask."

"I see from your papers that you live in Bucharest. What do you do there?"

"I am a student at the University of Bucharest at the Faculty of Mathematics."

"If that is true, why are you here in Arad?"

"I guess we are free to travel. I have never been here, so I wanted to see the city."

"You do not fool me," he said with a smile, as he was sure he caught me in a lie. "I know that you Baptists like to go to churches all over the country, so perhaps you visited some church this Sunday."

"Indeed, we Baptists do that. I have visited many churches in many cities."

"What church did you visit yesterday?"

Now I was in trouble. I could have lied and named some church in Arad, but if he wanted to pursue the subject, the lie would have been easily discovered. He could have asked me where the church was or who was preaching there, and I had no prepared answer.

"As a matter of fact, I did not visit any church."

"You lie to me," he said. "You are a Baptist who goes to church on Sundays. You live in Bucharest, you travel to Arad and do not go to church Sunday morning. That is not credible."

"It may not be credible, but that is the truth."

Now he tried another angle.

"Where did you stay in Arad?"

Since I slept two nights in the city, once in Ovidiu's house, once in an unknown person's apartment, I decided to stick to the latter.

"I stayed in the apartment of another Baptist believer."

"What is his name? What is the address?"

"You may not believe me, but I do not know." Indeed, I did not know, as the believer took me to his home late at night and I did not know what his address was.

"You are playing games with me," the captain said with irritation in his voice.

"I am not playing any games. I am telling you the truth," I protested. "I really need to catch this flight. Today at noon I have an exam and I do not want to miss it."

"Here is what we will do. I will give you a few minutes to think while I resolve some other matters. When I come back, you will give me honest answers. Otherwise, you stay here until this matter is resolved. Forget about your flight." With that, he stepped out of the office.

If I stayed there another ten or fifteen minutes, I would miss the flight. I had never skipped an exam, and, if I did, the consequences would have been quite unpleasant. That was not my main concern. I was more worried of the possibility of going through a long and hard interrogation. I had no experience with interrogations and I really did not know how I would perform. For the moment, I could use the flight to Bucharest to create some sense of urgency, but once the flight left without me, the police would have all the time they wanted to interrogate me. What if either by fear or by some trick of the interrogators I divulged some secrets? What if I became the man who collapsed the whole ministry of the Navigators in Romania? What if people would be arrested because of me?

Lord have mercy. Please give me an idea.

Suddenly, a plan sprung into my mind. It was a risky one, and it might have failed in many ways.

The captain came back in the office and sat at the table across from me. "Did you have enough time to reflect?" he asked me.

"I did, and I will now answer your questions," I responded.

I had to make it plausible so he would have no reason to continue the interrogation.

"First," I started, "I will tell you why I was reluctant to answer. I've heard of cases in which our police harassed Baptists, although it has never happened to me. I know of people who were interrogated without reason and sometimes accused of absurd violations of the law. You can do that to me, but I would feel bad if other people, whose names I will give you, have to suffer simply because I mentioned their names."

"Do not worry about that. We do everything in accordance with the law. No one will suffer if he or she did not break the law."

"Very well, thank you, but I would like to ask you for another favor. I will answer your questions as fast as I can.

But you have to promise me that once I do, you will immediately let me go so I can catch the flight to Bucharest."

I believe he was also happy to conclude the episode after he achieved his objectives, so he said, "I give you my word as a police captain that I will let you go as soon as you tell me where you stayed and with whom you met."

"Thank you, comrade captain. I know you are a man of honor. I stayed with my friend Ovidiu. We had not seen each other in a long time, and so we wanted to meet."

With that, I gave him Ovidiu's full name and home address. He let me go, and I was the last passenger to board the plane. I was quite agitated. It happened to be the first time in my life that I flew, and in normal circumstances I would have just enjoyed the experience. However, I had to go through my math textbook, which I took with me to prepare for the exam. I had a whole week to study, which now was reduced to one hour during the flight from Arad to Bucharest. In reality, I did not even have that much time, as I was busy racking my brains to figure out the details of my next move.

I knew that the Navigator's conference was continuing that day at Ovidiu's house. If the police decided to go there and ask questions to verify my story, they might discover seven or more people inside, including some Americans. That would have been a disaster. I had to find a way to alert them so that they would have time to disperse or move the meeting to another location.

After we landed, my first priority was to call Ovidiu's house. I did not call from the airport, thinking that maybe the police in Arad had alerted the police in Bucharest, who could have watched me. Instead, I took the bus to the city, walked around some buildings trying to detect a possible surveillance, and then went to a public phone and called. Ovidiu's wife, Ligia, responded. There was a possibility that the police or the Securitate were listening, so I had to choose my words carefully.

"Hello, Ligia," I said. "I just wanted to tell you that I arrived and everything is OK."

"I'm glad to hear that," she said. "Please say hello to Ana."

"Of course. I also wanted to tell you that I was stopped at the airport because they found a Bible in my briefcase. They asked a lot of questions, and I told them that I slept at your house. I gave them your address, so it is possible that this morning some policeman may come to your house to verify my story. I wanted to tell you this so you are prepared and so that you will not be afraid if a policeman shows up."

"I understand well," she said. "We'll be prepared if the police show up here."

I breathed a sigh of relief. She obviously understood, and I was sure they would stop the meeting and the guests would leave. Weeks later, I found out that my prediction was correct. A policeman came around noon, requested to see the house register, a document in which the owner was supposed to record all visitors (in fact very few did it), and

164

asked if I had stayed with them overnight. The guests were no longer there, and my statements and Ligia's statements were in perfect agreement.

I rushed home, where I found Ana, pregnant in the ninth month and not feeling well. Unfortunately, I could not stay too much with her. I rushed to the University and entered the examination room at the last moment.

I am not really prepared for this exam. Lord have mercy.

No matter how good I was at math, I had little chance of success without thorough preparation. When I received the exam, I realized it covered subjects from a section of the course which I happened to know well. The problems we had to solve were not difficult. When later the grades were announced, I found I had received a perfect 10. It was surely not my skill, but God's grace for me.

When I arrived home that afternoon, Ana told me that her water broke and that the child would come soon. We called the hospital, and an ambulance showed up in less than an hour. I could not go with her, as in Romania, in those times, husbands were not allowed to assist at the birth. I stayed home and waited for the call, which came shortly before midnight. It was a women's voice, a nurse from the hospital.

"Mister Oara, congratulations, you have a son."

While I could not remember other exact dates for this story, this one is easy: April 10, the birthday of my first son.

***

In March of 1979, a group of workers from the city of Dobreta-Turnu Severin formed a union called The Free Trade Union of the Working People of Romania, led by a physician named Ion Cană. The purpose of the union was to defend the real rights of Romanian workers, unlike the unions that were totally controlled by the Communist Party. The official unions were often called "transmission belts," as their main mission was to promote the interests of the Party. The idea of a free union, unsubordinated to the Party, was a slap in the face of the Communist authorities. Soon after Radio Free Europe announced the formation of the union, about 2,400 people signed up to join.

One of the problems they faced was how to make public announcements about their existence, their principles, and their actions. Their communiques were read at Radio Free Europe, but they had to find ways to send them there without being caught.

At that time, a man whom I trusted and who trusted me came to my apartment one evening and handed me an envelope. He asked if I could send it to Radio Free Europe as soon as possible. He explained that it was a public announcement from the Free Trade Union. I accepted the envelope, not knowing initially what I was going to do with it. After the man left, I remembered that my father-in-law left me an emergency contact, a Vice Consul at the American Embassy. He was already warned that I might visit him, and, if that happened, he should receive me.

I realized that I was crossing a line. Up until that time, all my secret activities had to do with oppressed Christians or with Christian work. If I were caught and arrested, I could easily explain why I did what I did. Ultimately, all of our activities were in a way innocent, as we did not directly challenge the monopoly of power of the Communist Party. We were persecuted for being different, for keeping our faith and culture and tradition, not for any explicit opposition. The Free Trade Union, on the other hand, was a direct challenge to the regime. This was neither evangelism, nor discipleship, nor help for persecuted Christians, but purely a political action.

In the morning, I went to the American Embassy located on the Tudor Arghezi Street, close to the National Theatre and the Intercontinental Hotel, and not too far from the University. I was admitted to the consulate building, where I gave my name and asked to speak with the Vice Consul. There were many people in the lobby, most of them there for routine business such as getting a US visa. I was sure that somewhere in that crowd there was at least one Securitate informer. When I was invited to the Vice Consul office, this informer must have noticed me as one who was there for something other than a simple visa.

The Vice Consul was a young man, perhaps not more than five years older than me. He greeted me warmly and invited me to sit. I introduced myself, and he seemed to be aware of who I was, just as he was aware of many other people who were in trouble with the Communist regime. We had a pleasant conversation, and he told me about the Star Wars movie which depicted the struggle between good and evil. He was curious to hear about the situation of the Christians in the country and about the dissident movements. I spoke freely, as I did not expect the Securitate to have secret microphones in the room. If they tried, the Americans had enough technology to detect them.

167

Finally, I gave him the envelope and I explained what it was about. He seemed to be well-informed about the Free Trade Union.

Before I left, I told him that there was some risk that the Securitate would grab and possibly arrest me when I left.

"I can help you," he said. "There is an lesser-known exit from an inner courtyard of the Consulate. It does not go to the Tudor Arghezi Street, but to an obscure side street."

He came with me and opened the door of a tall iron fence. We said goodbye, shook hands, and I went out. There were a few people walking on the sidewalks, and none of them looked out of place, which gave me some hope. I started walking towards the Intercontinental Hotel, with all my senses tuned to the max. I turned on to the main street leading toward the hotel, thinking that the danger had passed. After a few yards, I noticed a policeman in the frame of a large door of a building. He was talking into a walkie-talkie held in his right hand, and his eyes were scanning the street in my direction. Then I saw him nod, place the walkie-talkie in his belt, and step to the middle of the sidewalk, ready to intercept me.

I continued to walk in his direction, and when I was about thirty yards away from him, I suddenly changed direction and crossed the street to the other side, without turning my head to observe the policemen, as I did not want to make it obvious that I was trying to escape. I started to walk faster, but I did not run. I expected that at any moment the policeman would shout from behind me or would grab my hand, but nothing like that happened. Finally, I arrived at Nicolae Balcescu Boulevard, in front of the Intercontinental. There were some bus stops there, with many people on the sidewalk waiting for their busses to come.

When the first bus stopped, I tried to look calm, bored, and uninterested, but at the last moment, when the doors started to close, I jumped in. As the bus departed, I went to the back, where I could see the traffic behind us through the window. Was there any car following us? If so, I would see if a car stopped at the same time as the bus when loading or unloading passengers. No, I could not discover anything suspicious. I jumped off the bus at the Roman Plaza, sure that it was over and that I could go back home.

As I started walking, a policeman in uniform appeared out of nowhere and approached me. "May I see your identification papers?" he asked. There was no sense in trying to run - that would have made things much worse - so I simple pulled my *buletin de identitate* and gave it to the policeman. He pulled a small notebook from his pocket and wrote down my name. "You are free to go," he said. Apparently, they only wanted my name and there was no intention at that time to arrest or interrogate me.

To this day, I cannot figure out how they were able to pursue and intercept me after I took a random bus and went a number of stops. How did they communicate with the policeman at the Roman Plaza? They had no way of knowing where I would step out of the bus.

These are real professionals, I thought. *I must be even more careful in the future.*

169

AN ACCIDENTAL DISSIDENT

***

The Suspect

From that time, the circle around me started to shrink.

One morning, after I stepped on to a bus to go to the University, I noticed two familiar faces in the crowd. *Where did I meet these men?* I asked myself, but I could not remember any social situation where I had encountered them. Was it at church? No - if so, they would have come and greeted me, as I was a known figure there, even having preached a few times. Okay, it did not matter.

I went to attend a lecture, and when I came out of the University building, I saw them again. One was eating a hot dog from a street stand, the other was reading a newspaper. Suddenly the lights went on: I was being followed.

Over the next days, I paid special attention to the people around me on the street or on the bus. Slowly, I was able to figure out their tactics.

The surveillance team consisted of three people who followed me on foot, as well as two indistinct cars, each with two people inside. The cars appeared and disappeared, depending on how I moved through the city. Occasionally, the people on foot disappeared, and I figured out that they would switch places with those in the cars to make the surveillance less obvious. There were two teams - one in the morning, one in the afternoon.

Wow, fourteen people have a full-time job to follow me, I thought. *I must be an important person.* Strangely enough, I got a little ego satisfaction from this.

Then I noticed some other signs. My phone at my apartment stopped working for several days, then started working again. During phone calls, I heard suspicious clicks on the line which I did not hear before. It was clear that somebody was listening to my conversations, so I was always careful not to divulge anything.

In the meantime, I had some fun with my followers. I played the escape game, trying to see if I could get rid of them. The most obvious tactic was to jump on or off a bus at the last moment before the doors closed. One time, a man followed me on to the bus, and when I jumped out, he was trapped inside. I saw him coming to the back window of the bus and looking at me, on the street, with some anger on his face. *Goodbye, have a nice journey.* However, in general, it was difficult to get rid of surveillance. Once, I spent a few hours going through Bucharest to no specific destination, trying hard to shake them off. When I thought I had succeeded, I relaxed, satisfied, only to notice them again after a few minutes.

There was once a meeting which I wanted to attend, and I really did not want the Securitate to know about my destination, so I had to get rid of them. On that occasion, I used a new method. I went to the University, where the main building had six exits, all on populated streets. I got inside at the Faculty of Mathematics entry, as if I were going to a lecture. I climbed the stairs to the fourth floor, which was almost empty, then walked through long and narrow corridors. If somebody was following me there, it would be impossible not to see him behind me. I went

172

around and descended the stairs on the opposite side of the building. It would have been difficult for them to watch all the exits, and besides, they expected me to come out at the same entry, at the Faculty of Mathematics. Once in the street, I jumped on the next bus and then spent another thirty minutes changing directions and trying to detect surveillance. I did not see any, so I went confidently to the meeting.

Perhaps the surveillance team got some scolding from their bosses. *Sorry for the inconvenience,* I thought. *It's like war, kill or be killed.*

***

I was not the only one followed at that time.

Pastor Pavel Niculescu was one of the signatories of the letter to the Belgrade Conference, and when the Securitate started an investigation against the group, he was the only one beaten. While the other five were polite and appeared to cooperate, he was confrontational and refused to answer their questions.

Pavel was a man of short stature who wore thick glasses. He seemed a frail man, but he packed a lot of energy and determination. We used to go to his church, located at the periphery of Bucharest, to hear his sermons, which were highly theological and intellectual. When under pressure, he used to issue a pseudo-threat to his persecutors: "Just wait and you will see what will happen to us."

The Securitate paid much more attention to him than me, as I was always trying to keep a low profile. He was followed everywhere, all day long, by large teams of agents. In his case, the surveillance was not hidden, but visible. They wanted not only to know what he was doing and who he was meeting, but also to intimidate him and prevent him from pursuing activities which the authorities perceived as a threat.

One time, after the Sunday morning service, he wanted to go and meet somebody in secret. He asked a church member to take him in his car.

"Can you lose the agents who follow me?" he asked.

"I believe I can. Get in my car, and I'll see what I can do."

A chase started, worthy of James Bond movies. First, the driver moved with the traffic. Then, he suddenly accelerated and started to perform a slalom, cutting in front of some cars and hiding on the side of a truck, but to no avail: two Securitate cars were able to keep up with him. He turned from street to street, but they were still behind him. Then he tried something else and started to move through a maze of narrow streets which were harder to navigate, but they were still behind him. Eventually, he got in trouble. He entered at high speed on a long and narrow street, only to realize it was a dead end. He had to stop where the street ended, and the two Securitate cars had to stop too, right behind him. Now they were all stuck. He had no way of turning or backing off, as the Securitate cars were blocking his car. It was a moment of embarrassment. He got out of the car, went to his pursuers, and said,

"Gentleman, would you be so kind as to back up?" "Sure, do not worry," they responded, as if they were just some polite strangers. In the end, Pavel and his driver realized they could not get rid of the pursuers, and Pavel gave up on going to the meeting.

One evening, Pavel went to meet somebody and left his house late, after 11 PM. He had a problem getting home, as the only way was to take a tram, but at that hour the trams were rare, maybe once every 30 minutes. He went to the tram stop and waited. It was a dark winter night, and it was raining.

Two agents in a Securitate car were watching him from across the street. They must have been annoyed performing pointless surveillance tasks at that hour of the night. It was obvious that their target was just waiting for the tram to go home. After about five minutes of waiting, the car moved next to Pavel, a window was rolled down, and an agent asked him:

"Mister Niculescu, are you waiting for the tram to go home?"

"Yes, I am."

"Well," said the agent, "it is late and now the trams are rare."

"I know that, but I have no other solution than to wait for the next one, whenever it comes."

"Mister Niculescu, we have to also wait for you. This is absurd. Will you please get in our car? We'll take you home."

So, the Securitate men were not always evil. Sometimes they had common sense and sensibility to their fellow men. Maybe that nice offer was made just for convenience, but maybe it was an act of kindness. Only God knows.

***

As the Securitate was watching and following me, I thought it probable that I would soon be detained, interrogated, or even arrested. I was less afraid of what they would do to me than I was afraid of myself. How would I react? What if, when pressed, I started to talk and divulge some secrets? What if I gave names, and people would be harassed and go to prison because of me? I knew how to act at school and at church. I knew how to have an intellectual argument. I knew how to negotiate with a street vendor. But I had no idea how to behave during an interrogation. Yes, I was detained and interrogated once at the airport in Timișoara, but that was short and the interrogator was mostly on a fishing expedition.

I remembered what a friend of mine, who was a psychologist, once told me. In his profession, he talked with Securitate officers, who told him something of a paradox: "When we try to break somebody, and he resists, we are tough with him, but we respect him. After he breaks and agrees to cooperate, we treat him well, but we despise him." The highest fear I had was that I would break and become a dirty rag in the Securitate's hands.

AN ACCIDENTAL DISSIDENT

***

Nicolae Steinhardt was a Christian living in Bucharest at that time. He was born in a Jewish family and was raised in the Jewish faith. In 1959, he was asked to give testimony in a kangaroo court trial against a former school colleague, Constantin Noica, who later became a known philosopher.

He was told that he had to show up at a Securitate location to discuss his testimony before the trial. In his book, *The Happiness Diary*, he tells the story of that day. As he was living his home, his father told him, "Do not be a scared Jew, do not shit in your pants."

The Securitate used all possible arguments to convince him to testify. There were rational arguments: "The suspect will be condemned anyway," "It is your duty to tell the truth," and many others. Then they used threats, but he held to his position, refusing to testify against his friend. During the long discussion, he had one thought: *I will not betray my friends*. He did not testify, but the Securitate took its revenge and he was sentenced to thirteen years in prison for "crimes of conspiracy against social order." In prison, he converted to Christianity and was secretly baptized in 1960. As an interesting follow-up, after he got out of prison, he became a monk in 1960 and later the staretz of the Rohia monastery.

I remember how once, when I held a total fast for a few days, my brain was continuously working to find good reasons to stop the fast and eat. In the same manner, when one is under unrelenting pressure to betray, a couple of "reasonable" arguments may tip the scale. It is a case of

177

"reason" versus moral instinct. Depending on the person, one or the other may win.

In contrast to Steinhardt's principle, "I will not betray my friends," another Christian (his name was Cure) told me that at his trial he was surprised to see a fellow Christian from his church testifying against him. Cure was found guilty and sentenced to many years in prison. After he got out of prison, he was travelling by train one day, when he met his accuser.

"Brother," Cure asked, "why did you testify against me?"

"Well, they told me that you would be sentenced to years in prison anyway, so my testimony made no difference. However, they told me that if I did not testify, I would also go to prison, so I accepted."

Now I asked myself, which one I will be? Would I betray my friends under pressure from the Securitate?

***

I decided to do something about the expected clash with the Securitate and prepare in advance. I went to the Faculty of Law and found their library, which I had access to as a University of Bucharest student. There I found a book with the title *Criminal Investigations* and I looked for the sections about interrogations.

I had some real fun with it. The text was referring to police and prosecutors vs. criminals, good guys vs. bad guys. The police and prosecutors aimed to pull the truth from the person interrogated, but I was taking the side of the criminals, trying to figure how to counter the tactics of the interrogators.

Method: the bad cop, good cop tactic. The "bad cop" is tough, shouts, curses, and threatens the criminal. The "good cop" is sweet and understanding, a real friend of the accused. The criminal may abandon the inner resistance and open his heart to him. After all, he wants somebody to understand his side and be friendly with him.

Counter-method: Do not fall for this. The good cop is as dangerous as the bad cop. Take advantage of him, try to get something like a small break or a glass of water, but do not spill anything. Be friendly and fake trust in the good cop, even tell him some insignificant extra stuff, without divulging any secrets.

Method: When the accused tells a true story, the details are many and vivid. When he invents some story, the details are few and the story sounds distant.

Counter-method: When you tell a true story and have nothing to hide, be very sketchy. When you tell a fake story, make it vivid, with lots of details.

Method: During the interrogation, ask questions on a subject, then skip to another subject or even a third subject. See if the criminal's answers to the first subject change. He may commit a mistake and tell you first that in the evening he saw a movie, but the second time that he visited a friend.

179

However, if the same exact words are used the two times, the answers may be rehearsed.

Counter-method: Think well and compose the fake story in minute details. If the interrogator returns to your story later, make sure you do not vary any detail of the content, but try to use other words.

Method: Watch the suspect's reactions to your questions. If he hesitates or stumbles while answering a question, keep pressing, as perhaps this is where he feels afraid and wants to hide something.

Counter-method: Control your demeanor. As much as possible, slow down and hesitate during easy questions, and give precise (and false) answers for the difficult ones.

Method: Know the suspect. Have some discussions with him which are not necessarily about the subject of the investigation. Try to find his strengths and weaknesses so you can use them later, at the crucial moments.

Counter-method: The interrogator is not your friend, so do not open up to him. If you are weak, show yourself strong. If you are strong, show yourself weak. If you are calm, show yourself nervous. If you are nervous, show yourself calm. The interrogator should be confused or totally misunderstand who you are.

On the last point, I decided to build a fictitious persona to put on before interrogators. I would appear as ignorant and not too bright. I would make them believe all I wanted was to live a comfortable life, the perfect picture of middle class mediocrity. If I happened to meet foreigners or other dissidents, it was just by chance. I was thrown in the middle of the action, but I was a passive actor. I would appear a little scared, as displayed bravery would make them believe I was a dangerous person. I would somehow be "surprised" by their interest in me, given the fact that presumedly they would have no reason to pay attention to me.

One big question I had to answer before anything happened was if I would lie during an interrogation. The "Do not lie" command was deeply ingrained into my mind from early childhood. I had learned from experience that telling the truth, even when inconvenient, would quickly resolve any tough situation in which I was involved. A few times, as a child, I had lied to my mother, then was tortured with remorse. Sometimes, before going to bed, I sheepishly went to her and confessed my sin, and she was wise to forgive me and praise me for telling the truth.

Now, as a Christian, I had more reason not to lie, but that left me with a dilemma. Suppose that when asked if I received a package with smuggled Christian books from a certain fellow Christian, I would have said Yes. That could have sent my brother to prison. Even silence would have not helped, as it would have been an implicit Yes. I sinned if I said Yes, I sinned if I said No, and I sinned if I was silent. What would Jesus have done? He never hid, he never lied. When interrogated by the high priests and Pilate, he was silent most of the time. However, he was a teacher and a prophet Who came to tell the Truth, not a lowly, less-important underground activist. Besides, I was not of the same caliber as Him.

I struggled with this issue, and in the end, I built my own theory, which I called the Higher Truth. Suppose I was asked the question, "Did X give you that batch of Christian books?" A simple No or Yes would be expected. One would be true, one would be false. If the true answer was Yes, and I said Yes, person X would be arrested. According to my Higher Truth theory, Yes would in fact be a lie, as it would tell our persecutors that we were afraid, that Christianity had no substance, that we were ready to betray when put under pressure. On the other hand, a No, while technically a lie, was expressing a higher truth. If the persecutor eventually found out that it was a technical lie, he would admire Christians for their courage and solidarity. If he found out the truth and confronted me, I would simply say, with dignity, "I lied to protect my brother."

I was not a theologian, nor an ethics expert, but the Higher Truth theory offered me a solution. Maybe other people found better solutions to this moral dilemma, but it was good enough for me.

***

I was now much more careful than before, but continued to do the same things.

An American visitor brought me a projector and three films - Christian documentaries of some kind. I only remember the one about the miracle of water, about how perfectly God designed it to support life. As my apartment had a large living room, I could accommodate twenty or thirty people at a time for a showing. I invited people from church and from other churches, and we had nice evenings watching the movies. After I used the new tool to the maximum, I handed it to another Christian to take to the city of Iaşi, in Moldova. I advised him that he should do what I did: show the movies to many people, then give it to somebody else to take to another city. I am sure that the projector and the movies circulated through the whole country. I do not know what happened to them in the end, whether they were eventually intercepted by the Securitate or if they just deteriorated and stopped working after much use.

***

I was like a soldier waiting in the trenches for the enemy attack. I knew it was coming, but not when and how.

On a spring morning, I left home to go to the University, but I had some other chores to perform in the city before the lecture. I went first to the post office to send a telegram to my sister-in-law in Switzerland. She was a relay in a longer chain of communication that ended at different points in the West. It was convenient, as it was easier to send the telegram to a relative than to an organization with some hot title like "The Center for the Study of Communism and Religion." I was only using the telegram method in case of emergencies. In this case, I communicated that a certain dissident was arrested. The clerk at the post office gave me a copy of the telegram I sent, and I put the copy in my pocket, which, in retrospect, was a big mistake.

From the post office, I went to pay the utility bills - first electricity, then gas. I got receipts and I put those in my pocket too.

There was still some time before the lecture, and I decided that, rather than going to the University so early, I would go to the American Library, which was not far from the University building. I spent about half an hour there, after which I went to class.

At noon, I got out of class and headed toward the National Theatre, intending to take a bus home. I saw three men on the sidewalk ahead of me, but I did not pay too much attention. They were forming a perfect triangle, with the base towards me. When I was in the middle, they grabbed me. One of them opened the back door of a car waiting on the street next to us and pushed me inside.

It only took me a few seconds to understand what was happening: I was being "kidnapped" by the Securitate. I did not even bother to ask who they were and why I was abducted, as I knew well the answer. They had some trivial conversations but did not otherwise talk to me. After about fifteen minutes, the car stopped at a district police station, a modern building, and I was taken inside to a large lobby where policemen in uniforms and civilians were coming and going. After a few minutes, they took me to another large room, and I was asked to take a seat at a table.

As I was waiting, I racked my brains trying to figure out what was the immediate reason for my detention. There could have been many. Was it the movie I showed to many people at my apartment? Was it the telegram I had just sent that morning? Was it my visit to the American Embassy?

Finally, a young man dressed as a civilian came in and sat at the opposite side of the table. He introduced himself as a Securitate lieutenant, and, not remembering his name, I will call him here the Lieutenant. He was not much older than me, maybe in his late twenties or early thirties. He had the body of a gymnast, thin and fit. He seemed to be a sharp and intelligent fellow, and in another life he could have been my friend.

"Why do you think we brought you here?" he asked.

I was not stupid to answer that question. Would I be so naïve as to tell them that they detained me for taking a communique of the Free Trade Union to the American Embassy to send to Radio Free Europe?

"I really do not know. In fact, I was about to ask you the same question."

"We brought you here because you are involved in many treasonous activities which could end you up in prison."

"I am sorry to hear that. I am not aware of such activities, and I would never commit treason against my country," I protested.

"We know better. Do not try to play innocent."

After a few more general questions, he started to be more specific.

"What were you doing at the American Library this morning?" he asked.

I had a sigh of relief, as that was an easy one. Clearly they thought I was meeting some American contact at the Library. Maybe they thought this was a method to send messages to the West.

"Almost nothing. I was there only to kill time before going to a lecture."

"We do not believe you. You were there to meet somebody or to pass some message."

"I'm sorry you believe that. It was not the case."

"In that case, can you tell me what exactly you were doing inside?"

"I just browsed through some magazines and books."

"Are you sure? Do you want to stand by your statement? Do not forget that we have eyes and ears, and you cannot lie to us."

"Yes, I maintain my statement about what I did at the Library."

At that moment, another officer came into the room and introduced himself. This one was The Captain, a man in his mid-thirties. He seemed tougher and meaner than the Lieutenant. The two officers stepped aside, and I saw the Lieutenant briefing the Captain about what we discussed so far.

The Captain came to me and said, "I understand that you do not want to tell what you did at the American Library. Do you know the consequences?"

"I do not know the consequences, but whatever they are, I do not deserve them, as I am telling you the truth."

He looked angry. He brought some paper and a pen and placed them in front of me.

"You must write here EVERYTHING you did inside the Library," he told me in a threatening voice. "Do not leave out anything. Write to the lowest level of detail. I'll give you half an hour. When I come back, if I discover any lie, you'll be in big trouble. Understood?"

"Yes, sir, I will do exactly what you have requested."

With that, they stepped out of the room, and I was left alone. I was afraid, but I was also amused. *This will be delicious,* I thought, and I started to write. I tried to be neat, not make any mistakes, and use clear and even beautiful handwriting.

STATEMENT

Written by Ioan Mihai Oara on the date of … at the hour…

This morning at around 9:30, I came by bus from the direction of the Union Plaza and stepped out of the bus at the stop next to the Intercontinental Hotel. From there, I walked to the American

Library. At the entrance, I checked the schedule, so I could know when else I could come during active hours. I opened the door and entered inside. In the lobby, there was a receptionist seated at a table, and I said, "Good morning." She answered back and said, "Good morning."

I realized it was warm inside and I felt uncomfortable with my overcoat. I turned to the receptionist and asked if they had a coat room where I could leave my overcoat. She indicated that indeed they had a small room for that purpose, so I went there, took off my overcoat, and placed it on a hanger.

After that, I went to the magazine section and checked to see what magazines they had. I found a *Newsweek* with an attractive cover. On the cover was the title of an article inside, but I do not remember what it was. I started to browse through the magazine, and I stopped at an article about ice-cream. The point of the article was that ice-cream in America came in large varieties, perhaps hundreds. You could find vanilla, chocolate, and many other flavors. On top of that, they could be sprinkled with many artifacts, such as peanuts....

... and so on and so forth, for about six pages. In fact, I was not done when the two officers came back to the room.

I protested: "I'm sorry, I am not done yet."

"Don't worry," responded the Captain, "we just wanted to see what you wrote so far, then we'll give you more time to write."

He started to read with the air of a professional analyst studying an important document. As he progressed, his face showed more and more disgust, which later changed to anger. His face turned red.

"What did you write here? How did you dare? Do you think you can make fun of us?"

"Why?" I asked innocently.

"You know damn well why," he shouted. "You know we are not interested in this garbage. Tell me, did you intend to mock us?"

"No way, sir," I answered defensively. "You asked me to include every single detail. I do not know what you expected from me. Imagine I only wrote that I did nothing important. Would you then have been angry at me?"

He calmed down.

"Very well, then. Let me see your briefcase."

I opened the briefcase, and fortunately the only content consisted of a few math books and notes from the lectures. He picked up the notebook and started to browse through the pages. He frowned and seemed a little confused. The pages were filled with symbols unknown to him. There were differential equations, integrals and series.

"What is this?" he asked. Perhaps he thought it was some secret code.

"These are just equations," I responded. "If you want, I can explain them, but that would take some time, if you do not have a math background."

He seemed confused and suspicious, but the Lieutenant approached him and whispered, "It's okay, he is a math student."

"Fine," agreed the Captain. "Now empty your pockets."

I put my right hand in my pocket, and suddenly I realized that this could be my downfall. I remembered that I had two pieces of paper which could get me in big trouble.

The first one was the copy of the telegram which I sent to my sister-in-law in Switzerland, announcing the arrest of a dissident. Fortunately, if they discovered it, I would be the only one to suffer. My interrogators would have hard proof in their hands, which would come very handy in a possible trial. They would get their praises and promotions built on my downfall.

The second incriminating document was a note I wrote containing names, addresses, and money amounts for the funds I was distributing. Distribution of funds received from the West may have been illegal, if practiced on a large scale. Some names were crossed out, signaling that the money had already been given to the recipient. I would be asked who gave me the money, when, and for what purpose. The Securitate would then visit each person whose name and address appeared on my paper. Some would be trapped, some would be harassed or even arrested. Poor Mister Brătianu, who was so careful to refuse the money to avoid any incrimination, would be visited by the Securitate and asked why he received money from the West. His family was a pariah and the Securitate would have a great day finding an accusation against him.

All of that flashed through my mind in the second that it took to move my hand to my pocket. *How could I be so negligent?* Like most "criminals," I started my activities by being careful, but then I became lax. Initially, I always anticipated what could happen if I were caught, and I took the appropriate countermeasures. Do not take sensitive documents to dangerous situations! Have a cover story when you travel to another city for an important but secret meeting! In time, I started to slip here and there. I was like a driver, who after becoming experienced, is a little too self-confident and less careful on the road.

For a moment, I thought of swallowing the papers. It would have been difficult, as my pocket was full and I did not know where the incriminating documents were placed. This would look like a desperate act, and my false pretense of an innocent and ignorant young man would have been blown up. Worse, they could make me vomit or take other unpleasant actions to recover the papers.

I placed the stack of papers on the table and left it in God's hands.

The Captain took the first paper, looked at it, and asked: "What is this?"

I looked and answered, "It is a shopping list written by my wife."

He set it aside and moved to the next one.

"What is this?"

"It is a schedule of my classes at the university."

"What is this?"

"A Bible verse which I tried to memorize."

"And this?"

"The same, another Bible verse."

"What is this?"

"Receipt from my electricity bill payment."

"What is this?"

"This is a receipt of my gas payment."

The Captain looked bored and annoyed. He was looking for something significant, not for stupid receipts. He had to make progress and not waste his time in trivialities.

"Good. Put all the papers back in your pocket."

I was saved! I thanked God in my mind, and I could not avoid the thought that some disorderliness may be useful sometimes. If I were a well-organized person, my pocket would have contained just the bills, the copy of the telegram, and the money distribution list.

He invited me to sit. No doubt a long interrogation was about to start.

"You should know," the Captain said, "everything that is discussed or done here is a state secret. You are not allowed to tell anybody anything."

I almost smiled.

"Comrade captain," I said, "you abduct me from the street, you search me, you shout at me. You have all the power and you have many weapons. I only have one defense: to tell everybody everything that happens to me. I can tell you in advance that I will not keep any secret. On the contrary, I will tell everything."

"You are not allowed!"

"Moreover, as I will tell all my friends about this, I will have no control over this information. Do not blame me if this interrogation is announced at Radio Free Europe."

"I warned you," he said, unconvincingly.

He shifted uncomfortably in his chair and continued.

"I will ask now some questions to which you must give truthful answers. Remember, you cannot lie to us, we know everything about you."

Sure, they knew a lot - after all, they followed me and listened to my phone. Perhaps some of their informants wrote *note informative*, in which they described some peripheral details about me, but I was confident that they did not know the heavy stuff which really mattered for them.

"In that case, I see no reason why you would ask me these questions. Maybe you should let me go home. My wife must be worried because I did not appear."

After saying this, I immediately regretted it. I did not want to infuriate him further to my detriment, but he only said, "Do not be smart with me."

"What is your relationship with Pavel Niculescu?" he asked.

"We are friends. He is a good preacher and sometimes I go to his church just to hear him speak."

"What do you discuss when you meet?"

"We discuss Jesus, our faith, things like that."

"I'm sure you discuss much more, so answer truthfully."

"I do not have anything to add."

194

"You visited the American Embassy. Why?"

"There is a family in our church who intends to emigrate to the United States. I wanted to help them and find out if they could get a visa."

"You are lying again. You did not go to the counter where people usually go; you went into an office."

"That is correct."

"You see, we know everything. Who did you meet in that office?"

"Indeed, you know a lot. There is no point in hiding anything. I met the American Vice Consul."

"Why did you have to meet the Vice Consul, when this was a low-level inquiry to which any clerk at the consulate could have answered."

"You are right again," I responded, with a fake admiration for his perspicacity. "The reason was that when my father-in-law left, he told me that he met the Vice Consul, and if I had any problem I could go directly to him. Why bother with a low-level clerk when I could meet the boss?"

"What did he tell you?"

"He told me that in most probability the family would get the visa."

If I reported a conversation with a Romanian citizen, the Securitate could have interrogated him to find if there was any contradiction. In this case, I had no reason to worry. They could not interrogate the American Vice Consul.

"Did you discuss other subjects?"

"Nothing I can remember... Oh, I remember now. He told me about a great movie which runs in the United States, Star Wars."

For a short time, I took the initiative. It was obvious that they wanted to act in the shadows; they did not want their harassment of dissidents to be known. He was uncomfortable when I said I would tell everybody.

"Excuse me, comrade captain, I am not good with names. Can you tell me again what your name is?"

I suspected that if Radio Free Europe mentioned his name, he would be scolded by his superiors. On the other hand, it was standard practice for Securitate officers to disclose their names when dealing with a suspect.

"I will tell you my name," he said after a long pause. "But I do not want my name to be mentioned at certain radio stations."

I nodded but made no promise.

"Did you meet the priest Gheorghe Calciu?"

196

Here I felt a little more uncomfortable. I met him several times and we discussed sensitive issues. Moreover, I met his wife and passed money to her to help support his family after he was dismissed and arrested.

"Yes, I did."

"How, when?"

"My father-in-law brought him to our house one day."

"What did you discuss?

"I was with him only for a short while. He continued the discussion with my father-in-law, but if I remember correctly, I had to go to the University, so I was there only for a few minutes."

"What did you discuss?

"It was kind of theological. He is Orthodox, we are Baptists. Our churches are not in communion, and in general each one believes that the other is in error. However, Father Calciu was very kind and told us that in his opinion we can all be saved in our own churches."

"Anything else?"

"Not that I remember."

I was sure that he would come back to this, and I felt uneasy about it. I had to find a way to divert attention to other subjects.

"Two weeks ago, you were seen on a Sunday evening giving a book to a person in the church yard. We know who he was. What book was that?

It was true, I remembered. A few months prior to that event, an old member of our church had intercepted me after service and told me he was concerned because he heard that the Securitate had become unusually active in those days and may come to do searches at Baptists' homes. He had a book which he did not want to fall into the hands of Securitate and be used against him. He was asking me if I had a good way to hide it.

I looked at the book and was a little surprised, as I did not think it was something that would create any danger to its owner. It was innocuous, with a title like *The Light of the Gospel*, written by some third-rate American author. Somebody must have found it interesting, translated it into Romanian, and sent it in the country through one of the many secret routes. The man giving me the book to hide was either an agent provocateur or a naive and scared Christian. I thought it did not matter, and to calm his nerves, I took the book and simply placed it in a bookshelf in my apartment next to others which would have been more dangerous.

Two weeks prior to my interrogation, the man came back to me and told me that now he felt safe and maybe I could retrieve the book from my hiding place and return it to him. I did so promptly, and perhaps some informer thought he could earn some extra points with his master by reporting the act.

This last question was my perfect opportunity. I remembered my preparation and decided that now was the moment to lead them on a long track to a dead end. While, before, my answers were prompt, now I hesitated. I laid back on the chair and started to rotate my eyes as if some intense process was going through my mind.

"Why are you asking?" I responded with my own question.

"Because I can and because you must answer all my questions, immediately and without any lie."

"Am I not entitled to some privacy?" I tried again.

"You are not entitled to any privacy when it comes to criminal actions against the state."

"I did not do any criminal action against the State. However, I would like to skip this one."

"You cannot skip anything."

"Still, is there any law that forces me to answer all your questions?"

He stood up and struck the table with his fist and cursed me. The Lieutenant, who was absently reading some papers from a file, put them on the table and started to pay attention. Now they were getting somewhere! Maybe they had struck gold.

I was a little taken aback by the Captain's reaction and I made sure I showed it Perhaps my face even became white.

"Comrade captain," I said, almost stuttering. "I am perfectly willing to answer any question, I only wanted to …"

"I don't care what you want. Just answer the question."

"Yes, I will answer the question, but I wanted to explain to you that I do not want to involve other people in this. They are innocent, why get them in trouble?"

"Never mind, we already know who the person was. Now tell me what book it was."

"As far as I know, the Constitution of our country allows for the free circulation of books and ideas. I do not see how a simple book can be of such interest to you."

"We decide what is or is not of interest for us. Your obligation under the law is to answer our questions."

"Do I have to answer all questions, or only those which are relevant? After all, we all have some innocent areas of our lives which we like to keep private."

He pointed his finger to my face and shouted, "Never mind that. I am not getting into a philosophical discussion with you. Just answer the question. What book was that?"

"Yes certainly. It's just that I did not believe this to be of any interest. The book was titled *The Light of the Gospel*. Unfortunately, I do not remember the name of the author. Once, a teacher told me that I should always remember the names of the authors of the books I am reading, and I believe he was right. However, I am not good with names, I tend to forget them quickly. Somebody once told me a technique on how to remember names ..."

"I am not interested in your techniques," the Captain said in exasperation. "What was the book saying? What was it about?"

"The book explained how the world lies in darkness, but the Gospel is shedding the light and people can live in the light rather than in the darkness."

The Captain was on the edge of losing his temper. He asked me a few more questions, then started a long monologue. He told me that I stood accused of treasonous activities and that I would be crushed if I did not cooperate. He told me that he had total control over my fate, and if I wanted to avoid total destruction, I had better start giving him honest answers. Eventually, he worked himself up and started to curse me.

I can only vaguely remember the next hour or hours. I felt like a fortress under assault. The enemy was probing all the gates and sending arrows to kill all defenses. I felt weaker and weaker, and I had one single desire: that this interrogation should stop at once. I could feel that my strength was leaving me, and my only relief would be to submit and give him all he wanted so he would leave me alone. I was searching inside myself to find some hidden force, some leftover strength that would sustain me a little more, and I finally found it.

I started to sing in my mind some of the most beautiful Baptist hymns I knew, "How Great Thou Art", "Great Is Thy Faithfulness", and many others. In between songs, I recited psalms, which the Navigators were pushing us to learn by heart. Psalm 1: "Blessed is the man who…." Psalm 23: "The Lord is my shepherd." Slowly, the room and the two officers started to fade. My eyes were following the face of the Captain, but I was totally absent. Occasionally, I nodded, as if I understood what he was saying, but that was an empty gesture. I was floating in another world, of still waters and green meadows, of divine hymns and fatherly love from above.

I do not know how long this took, but it must have been at least an hour, if not more. I lost all sense of time, and to this day I cannot remember anything that went on in that time of reverie.

The Captain stopped, tired and exhausted, and stepped out of the room to take a break. I looked at my watch: it was past seven o'clock. I had already spent close to seven hours under interrogation.

An older man entered the room, approached the table, and introduced himself: "I am Colonel Ştefănescu." He extended his hand – something the other two did not do – and we shook hands.

He looked around sixty, had dark glasses, and was dressed in a modest suit. If I saw him on the street, I would have believed him to be a gentle pensioner going to wait in a line for meat in front of a store. However, it was clear he was a superior officer, much higher than the other two.

"How are you, Mister Oara?" he asked, and I was surprised when he called me Mister.

"As you can see, not too well," I answered. "My wife is probably worried by now, as I did not arrive home."

"Well, you must be tired, we are tired, so we can conclude this quickly."

This is the good cop, I immediately thought.

"I understand that you are not giving honest and complete answers to the questions," he continued in a calm voice. "In a way, I understand and even admire you. You Baptists think of yourselves as being Christians under persecution. Well, there is no Nero here to throw you to the lions. We are not against you as Christians. You can worship God as much as you like, you can go to church, sing your hymns and listen to your preachers. No problem at all."

He had a warm voice and looked friendly. He was the good uncle, the benevolent teacher, the wise man giving me free fatherly advice.

"The problem is this," he continued. "A lot of your people are deceived. There are people in the West who

203

want to attack our country, and the best way they found is to stir discontent among Christians. It is like Iago who whispered in Othello's ear that Desdemona was unfaithful. They were greatly in love, and could have been happy together, but Othello became jealous and killed her. This is what is happening here."

He paused to let me digest it.

"Please ignore the captain, he is a little hotheaded. You are an intelligent person - I know that by looking at your grades - and for that reason I want to have a nice rational discussion with you. I'm sure we can get along. We are all Romanians and we all love our country. Rather than listening to these insinuations of foreigners whose goal is to create discord, work with us for the common good. We have nothing against your faith. You can believe whatever you want. I see you are associated with some bad characters. Did you know that the priest Gheorghe Calciu was a fascist in his youth? Have you noticed that your friend Pavel Niculescu is unbalanced, to say the least? Are these the people you want as friends? Despite their foolishness, we do not want to harm them, all we want is to prevent acts which would harm our country, which we all love and intend to serve. You can do your patriotic duty by simply telling us what some of these misfits are doing. Nobody else will know. Moreover, we'll recognize your contribution and make sure that your future career is unimpeded. Occasionally, you'll need recommendations for certain jobs, or somebody will consult with us about you before hiring you or giving you a promotion. You will become a scientist or a university professor, and you'll be invited to various conferences, some of them in the West. We'll have to vouch for you to travel, and I will personally guarantee you will receive a positive review. So, what do you think?"

I was sure he wanted to provoke me to a long discussion, but I remembered my interrogation methods and counter-methods. He wanted to feel me, to test me, to discover my inner triggers, my fears, my weaknesses, my dreams, my desires, then find my weakest point and concentrate his superior skills towards it. I knew that the natural human desire to communicate with another human would be perverted in the service of an evil system. I knew this was not an encounter between a YOU and an I, but between a SUBJECT and an OBJECT, and I did not want to be that object. On my side, there would be no opening of the soul, no extended hand, no trust, and no dialogue beyond what was strictly needed.

"Comrade Colonel," I answered, "I believe you overestimate me. I am a simple student with little interest for politics. Some of these people I have met by pure chance, as they came to visit my father-in-law. I do not think I can help you, and I would rather not get involved in such things."

Unlike the Captain, he did not show any signs of frustration.

"There is another aspect of which I hope you are aware." he continued. "Between you and me, I have some admiration for Christians, although I do not say so publicly.. You see, in my profession, we must deal with all kinds of criminals. Some are real scum. But the Christians have some morals, some principles. Above all, they tell the truth. Yes, you should always tell the truth! It is in the

Bible, it is part of your faith. So, when we ask you questions, I expect you to tell me the truth, not because I force you in any way, but because I really want to continue to respect you. Have you thought about that?"

"Yes, we should all tell the truth," I answered, but I was thinking of my version of the truth.

"Are you now ready to tell us the truth about your activities and your contacts?"

"There is nothing to tell, and I would rather not go through that again."

There was a pause, and he looked at me, but not in a threatening way. Then, he stepped outside, and I was alone for a few minutes. He came back with a paper in his hands.

He said, "Here is what we will do. I am sure you are tired and want to go home. To tell you the truth, I also want to go home." He smiled. "I have a statement I would like you to read and sign. I hope you will find it acceptable.

I read it with utter attention to detail. It went something like this:

I, the undersigned, Ioan Mihai Oara, student in the 4th year at the Faculty of Mathematics of the University of Bucharest, after a discussion with staff of the State Security, promise the following:

I will not initiate or participate in any illegal action that endangers the security of the state.

206

Moreover, if I become aware of such activities, I will immediately and without hesitation report them to the organs of the State Security apparatus.

Signed,

....

Pavel Niculescu would have not signed it, but I found it acceptable for several reasons, the main one being that it was vague on what constitutes an "illegal action that endangers the security of the state." Paradoxically, 99% of my activities were not illegal in a strict interpretation of our laws. The Constitution of Romania specified the freedom of religion, of conscience, and of free association. The exact word was "guarantees," and in various political lectures, we were told that while Capitalist constitutions only specify these rights, our Socialist constitution guarantees them. It was, of course, pure propaganda, but I could hang to these words. When we distributed Bibles, secretly met for discipleship sessions, or refused to sign an oath of allegiance to the Party, it was all legal, at least according to the Romanian Constitution.

There were a tiny number of activities that may have fallen into the "illegal" side, but even for these, the question was, were they directed against state security? It was all a matter of interpretation. Was the Romanian state in danger if I handed people books which claimed that Marx was a Satanist, or, not being able to complain publicly, I secretly sent a message to Radio Free Europe announcing that the authorities had demolished a church? No, only the Communist regime was in danger of being exposed as an oppressor and hypocrite. In fact, telling the world what was happening was only increasing the respect of other countries for a people who dare to oppose an authoritarian regime.

I was also sincere when I signed that I would inform the authorities about dangers to the state, and here I had again my own interpretation. If I found out that there was a Hungarian conspiracy to take back Transylvania, I would have certainly reported it. If I accidentally intercepted a message showing that the Soviet Union intended to invade us, I would have immediately and without hesitation taken it to the competent authorities. But if Pavel Niculescu said in a meeting that Communism would not last forever, I would not report his words.

Yes, I will sign.

"You are free to go," said the colonel. "Greetings to your wife and my apology for keeping you so long. I would like, however, to continue a friendly discussion with you tomorrow. Can you come back, let's say at ten in the morning?"

I could not say no, so I accepted, gathered my things, and left. It was night outside. I could have taken the bus home, but I decided to walk to clear my mind.

Suddenly, I was filled with a feeling of euphoria. I survived. Not only did I survive, but I kept my dignity. I remained a free person. I could tell my wife, my friends, and later my children about what happened that day.

When I arrived home, I was glad to find that Ana was not sick with worry She was sure that I would come home sooner or later. I spent a few hours into the night telling her about my interrogation.

***

The next day, I went again to the police building for another discussion with the colonel. He was polite, and there was no more hard pressure to cooperate. He alluded a couple of times to the great benefits of working together, but I remained unmoved, at the same time trying not to provoke him. Then he started to tell me about himself, perhaps hoping that if he opened up and talked about himself, I would do the same, in a natural human reaction.

"When I was young, just like you, I had to make certain choices, but I took a path different from the one you chose. I was a young officer, assigned to a unit that was fighting anti-Communist partisans in the mountains. It was a heroic time. I was involved in firefights and my life was often in danger. I did this out of a sense of duty and love for my country."

I knew about that era from various secret publications. There were people, sometimes whole families, who decided to fight with weapons the Communist regime installed by the Soviet troops. They were chased and annihilated one by one.

The typical story was about a partisan who came at night into a village to get some milk. The Securitate found out from some informer and waited for him in darkness. When he was cornered, he took refuge in a barn, and the Securitate soldiers set it on fire. When he came out, they shot him dead.

209

I kept a poker face, showing neither approval nor disapproval, continuing my tactic of not disclosing any of my feelings or thoughts. In the end, he came with a surprise proposal.

"I know that your father-in-law emigrated to America. Have you ever thought of joining him there?"

"No, it never crossed my mind," I responded.

"Well, think about it. It may be a good idea. If you decide to go, we'll approve it. You'll have no difficulty in getting a passport for you and your family."

With that, he let me go.

The Dissident

While I was determined to continue all my prior activities, I had to slow down, not out of fear, but because I had to work on my graduation thesis.

Although my first love was algebra, I decided to pursue mechanics in my last year, thinking that it would make it easier for me to get a job, given my not-so-favorable Securitate file. Algebra had fewer applications, and I thought I could use mechanics in some state enterprise which needed engineers and scientists.

My thesis supervisor was Professor Nicolae Cristescu, a man I greatly respected. He must have been in his late forties and had several books published in Romania and abroad. He had a big mustache, making him look older than he was, but also giving him the appearance of a benevolent grandfather.

One day, after a seminar, he pulled me aside and told me: "Oara, I was asked to keep a special eye on you as a 'trouble' student, but, have no fear, I will support and help you as much as I can."

I was grateful when he told me that. It was refreshing to find a man who did not bendunder the will of the Party but continued to do what he believed to be right.

Most students prepared their thesis by presenting some aspects of a math theory, which they picked from books. I asked Professor Cristescu to suggest to me something more challenging. He told me that there were some aspects of viscoplasticity not yet fully researched, and I could pick something in that area. The narrower subject was that of metal extrusion, the process used in manufacturing metal pipes.

As I worked on my thesis, I realized that I bit off more than I could chew. There were complex equations with partial derivatives, which were notoriously hard to solve. However, I later realized that, while a general solution is hard to find, in special cases solutions are possible. I found that a particular representation of the functions involving pressure, movement, and the specifics of the metal makes it possible to solve the equations. I then proceeded to write the thesis, which was not a trivial task, as everything had to be written neatly by hand at a time when we did not have personal computers with word processors.

I submitted my theses and then sustained it in front of a commission, in which Professor Cristescu was a member. He praised my research and pointed out that my results were original. I got the maximum grade.

I graduated and received my diploma in June of 1979. The threat of Antonie Iorgovan to have me expelled from the university did not come to pass.

***

After graduation, I started to think seriously about Colonel Ştefănescu's suggestion. Should we try to emigrate to the United States? My dream and my calling were always to become a mathematician, but it was not possible achieve this in Romania, where I would not be accepted for a PhD due to my bad political file. Although I was active on the religious scene, leading Bible studies and even preaching at times, I did not intend to become clergy. Also, my association with dissidents and various secret activities was an accident driven by circumstances, not something I considered to be a life purpose.

There were other issues involved. Ana discovered she was pregnant again, and we would soon have a second child. Wouldn't they be better off growing up in a free society? What would happen if I were dismissed from all jobs and not able to support them? A common tactic of the regime was to have an undesirable person fired, blocked from any employment, then accused of parasitism and sent to prison. As a math graduate, I would normally work as a teacher in a school, but the regime did not like to have declared Christians as teachers, so my career would most probably be a short one.

There were, at the same time, reasons not to emigrate. Although Colonel Ştefănescu promised that if we applied for a passport we would be approved, I could not fully rely on his promise. If our application was rejected, I would have never gone back to him, saying, "You promised. Now can you help me?" He would have certainly asked for something in return and then used it to squeeze me.

The most serious reason to stay was my parents. Our emigration would have meant that they might never see us or their grandchildren again. I travelled to Alba Iulia and discussed the subject with them. They told me to go. My mother was strong and cared more for our future than for her old age. I knew that our happiness and our welfare would make her happy.

In the end, we decided to go.

Even before we applied for a passport, we had a country-level meeting of the Navigators, which I hosted in my apartment. At the end of the meeting, I announced my intention to emigrate to the United States. It was not well received. Some of my best friends looked at it as an abandonment of my work and of the investment which the Navigators had made in me. I felt better when one of the American Navigators said, "It's okay. We do not invest in geography, we invest in people."

***

Finally, I took the first decisive step which was would launch us towards an unknown future. One day, during the summer, I went to the police station that dealt with passport applications. There was a large lobby, full of people. Some of them were waiting in a long line to determine the status of their submitted applications. A policeman, bored and annoyed, was responding from behind a window.

"Your application was rejected. Sorry, I cannot do anything about it."

"There is nothing new, you have to wait."

"But I have already waited for three years."

"Go home and wait some more."

On a table, there were separate piles of forms one had to fill out to apply for a passport. Everybody knew that there were two steps in the process. There were two sets of forms, known as the small forms and the large forms. One had to apply first using the small forms. Perhaps 95% of the applications were stuck there. The applicant had to wait for years, during which his life would become hell. He would be called to the police station and given a strong warning to withdraw his application. If he refused, he would be called into a meeting where he worked, and he would be criticized and again asked to withdraw his application. If he still refused, he would be in danger of being fired, which frequently happened. He and his family would be left in limbo. He would lose any chance for promotion at his job. Some applications were approved on the basis of family reunification, when a husband already in the West declared a hunger strike and showed up with banners in front of Romanian Embassies in Paris or Washington. I had no intention to go through that process, but I left it in God's hands. If the application was not approved, so be it. My political status was already so bad that an application for a passport would not make it worse. I would apply and just go on with my life.

The authorities were alarmed at the large number of people applying for passports to emigrate. Besides the harassment of the applicants, they also tried propaganda. One day that summer, I read a story in the Party's main newspaper, *Scânteia*, which I will try to summarize here.

Cristian Iuga was an esteemed surgeon in Bucharest. He had a nice apartment with three bedrooms on Calea Victoriei, a car, a wife, and two children. He earned a good salary. He listened to certain foreign stations which were spewing their lies claiming that life is much better in a capitalist country. He applied for a passport and soon received it, although his colleagues warned him he was making a great mistake.

He arrived in Paris with some money in his pocket and was able to rent an apartment in a poor section of the city. For months, he could not find a job. Eventually, he was hired by a hospital, not as a surgeon, but as a janitor, washing the floors. He could hardly live on his small salary. When his child was sick, he could not even buy the appropriate medicine for him.

After a few months, his boss called him and told him that he must work more hours at lower pay. He complained, but his boss told him to shut up, because there was no Communist Party Secretary to fight for his rights there. His wife and child were crying, saying that they could not continue like that.

He went to the Romanian Embassy and asked if he could come back. The embassy gave him the proper documents and helped pay for his tickets to fly back to Bucharest. After he returned, he was immediately reinstated as surgeon in the hospital where he worked. The healthcare workers received him with love.

Of course, nobody believed the story.

I picked up the appropriate forms and started to fill them: name, address, family, dates of birth, parents,

parents' addresses, brothers and sisters and their addresses, profession, education, current job, address of the current job, supervisor, supervisor's phone number, any criminal record, current salary, and so on and so forth. There was a special space with the heading "Reasons for Leaving the Country." Since my in-laws were already in the United States, I simply wrote "Family reunification."

Next to me was a young man filling out his application. When he arrived at "Reason for Leaving the Country," he turned to me and asked, "What the heck should I write here?" I recognized from his tone that he was that type of character who did not take things seriously, a cynical bohemian.

"How should I know?" I said, indifferently.

"What did you write?"

"Family reunification. I have my in-laws in America."

"That does not go for me. I do not have any relatives abroad."

He sighed and paused to think, as if waiting for some muse to inspire him, then a wicked smile broke on his face.

"I know," he said, "I will write, 'I'm hungry'."

***

One morning, I picked up the mail and found an unpleasant letter from the city.

217

The building in which you live was found
unstable after the 1977 earthquake. The city has
decided to renovate it. You are required to make
your apartment available for repairs starting at 8 in
the morning on the date of …

We had no choice. The city could do whatever it
wanted; it was their property. There was no chance to
oppose the decision. There was a family living in the
apartment above us who opposed the renovation, and a
family living below us who pushed for the renovation.
They were in a continuous battle on this subject, each using
their ways to influence the city in its decision. Once, the
man below talked to me about the ongoing battle.

"I know how to defeat them. It is just a matter of
pulling strings at the right place and at the right level of
authority. If I only knew who his man at the City Hall was,
I would immediately go one level up and my man would be
more powerful than his." In the end, the neighbor above
won, and we had to prepare for the major renovation of the
building.

The trouble was that I had my wife with a three-
month-old baby who could not live in an apartment under
renovation. I found a family of friends who graciously
offered to host them, while I stayed behind to ensure that
nothing was stolen or destroyed.

Nobody came to start work on the appointed date, nor
on the second or third day. Eventually, the bell rang one
morning and three workers showed up, announcing that
they would start the work. The first thing they did was to
take the plaster off the walls, making an incredible mess

and filling the apartment with dust. It was a one-day job, after which they disappeared. I waited a day, a week, a month, nothing! I made phone calls, but nobody knew anything.

Eventually, they came back and started work in earnest. I was on friendly relations with them, and we often talked. I told the team leader that this apartment used to belong to my in-laws, who had emigrated to United States, and that I also intended to go there. He looked at me disapprovingly.

"Mister Oara, why do you want to emigrate? How can you leave your fatherland, where you were born and grew up, and go to a foreign country?"

"It's because of you," I responded.

His jaw dropped. "What do you mean because of me?"

"Because you came here, took the plaster from the walls, made a mess, and then disappeared for a month. What kind of country is this? How can I live here?"

He sighed and went back to work.

When the renovation was finished, after another two weeks, I brought Ana and our child back to the apartment. Life seemed to return to normal, until, one morning, a gentleman came to our door.

"My name is Ioan Zidaru," he said. "I have here a paper from the city which allocates two bedrooms in this apartment for my family."

There was nothing I could do about it. In general, a family with one child would get a one-bedroom apartment, at most. With two or three children, maybe they could get a two-bedroom apartment. Families had to wait years to have an apartment allocated to them, and when that happened, it was an apartment at the periphery. Yet, Ana, our child, and I had an extra-large, elegant, four-bedroom apartment in the center of Bucharest.

Ana did not take the news about our new situation well. No, she could not live in the same apartment with another family, sharing the only kitchen and the only bathroom. She had a small baby and she wanted cleanness and silence. I agreed with her, and in the next days, I racked my brains trying to find some solution.

The solution came in the form of a complex move. Mr. Zidaru had a brother who lived with his family in a three-bedroom apartment, in a distant corner of Bucharest called Berceni. The move was this: Mr. Zidaru and his family would take our apartment, which he would occupy together with his brother's family. Ana and I would move to his brother's apartment; not only us (we might have not been entitled to a three-bedroom), but also her sister Magdalena's family, which consisted of her, her husband, and a child of the same age as our son. With this move, all families received the space to which they were entitled, and there was no danger that some stranger would show up with a new allocation. Magdalena's husband, Tudor, worked in Oltenita, a town on the Danube, about fifty miles from Bucharest, so he would only be occasionally present. This arrangement gave us another advantage: the new apartment was in walking distance to the school where I was supposed to start working in the fall.

I was sad to leave our apartment, the place where I proposed to Ana and where we held so many meetings, some secret and some less secret. Our standard of living was taking a hit, but only for a short time, as we hoped to get the passports and emigrate.

***

The best students who graduated with me continued their study at the graduate level. I would have been among them, but that did not make sense for me as I expected to emigrate. I had to take a job, at least for a time.

The job allocation system upon graduating college in Romania was equitable. Everybody got a job, willing or not. The number of available jobs for each department's graduates was equal with the number of graduates. The jobs were listed in the University's halls, and before the job placement day, the graduates came, looked at the list, and tried to select the ones which they could realistically choose. On the placement day, the students were called in front of a commission in decreasing order of their grades. The top student could choose anything he or she wanted. The next one had the rest of the list to choose from, and so forth. The students at the top picked the best jobs in Bucharest, while those at the bottom were left with some poor jobs in remote villages.

There were about twenty positions in Bucharest, another twenty or thirty in major cities, and the rest in small

towns or villages. Placed at the top, I could choose from any of these. After some careful research, I picked School 98 in Bucharest.

I showed up at the school around September 1st, after about a twenty-minute walk from my new apartment. I was received by the principal, who had an unusual name. His last name was Ionescu, perhaps the most common last name in Romania, but his first name was Napoleon, which was quite unusual. He was in his mid-forties and wore a smile showing that he was amused by the people or the situations he encountered.

He invited me to sit, welcomed me, and expressed his hope that we would have a good relationship. I reciprocated, but also considered it my duty to give him a few warnings about me: I was a practicing Christian and I had an application for emigration. I did not know if or when it would be approved. "No problem with me," he said.

Being a teacher was a new experience for me, and I had some fun with it, in spite of the fact that it was not my dream profession. I loved my students and tried in earnest to help them understand and practice math at their level. Although education was one of the strong points of Romania, I felt that, even here, the hand of the Party manifested in many ways. Ceaușescu disbanded all schools for children with special needs, as he thought that their existence lowered the prestige of the country. Officially, we did not have any children with mental deficiencies. I ended up with one case of a mildly retarded boy and of one whom I believed to be schizophrenic, often disruptive during the classes.

At the end of one semester, the principal announced that the Party did not tolerate any cases of students failing classes. If that happened, the blame fell on the teacher, who would have to forfeit his vacation and spend it at school, tutoring the failing students. Because of this directive, teachers inflated the grades to make sure there were no failures. I almost got in trouble with this, as one of my students in the seventh grade stopped coming to school and I found to my horror that, according to his grades at that point, he would fail.

I could stand on the side of reason and justice, and fail him, but that was not my fight. There were so many bad things in the country, and I could not protest everything. My focus was on my Christian underground activities. I sent word through other children to this failing student to come to school, with the explicit message that my intention was to help him pass.

He finally showed up to one class, and I hurried to examine him before he disappeared again.

"Listen, Marius," I told him, in front of the class, "I know you do not like algebra too much, but I can demonstrate to you that it is not so difficult after all. Please come to the board and I will ask you to answer some questions. You will see how easy it is."

He came in front of the class, totally indifferent to the danger of failing. I wrote on the board: $5x+7x = \_$. "What is the result of this calculation?"

He looked dumbly at me, as if saying "I have no idea."

"Let's try something simpler," I said, and wrote on the board 2x+3x= _. He was still lost, so I had the idea to use my fingers to make it more intuitive.

"Here you have 2x. It does not matter what x is - it could be one of my fingers." I raised my hand, closed my fist, then extended two fingers. "So now you have two fingers, but then you add another three." I extended the other fingers and I showed him all five. "Now, how many fingers do you have?"

"Five," he answered, but only after a short hesitation.

"Bravo, Marius!" I exclaimed. "You see, you can be good at math, all you need is to use your brains. Excellent, keep doing that and you'll be soon a pro." I gave him a passing grade.

**

Sometime in December, before the end of the first semester, a Communist Party meeting was announced, at which all teachers must be present. Not all teachers were Party members, and there were members-only meetings, but this was, as it was called, an "enlarged" meeting.

I went, not knowing what it was about. At the front table sat the principal, a lady who was the local Party organization secretary, and yet another lady who was taking the minutes of the meeting.

The principal opened the meeting by telling us that the Communist Party decided to raise all transportation costs in

Bucharest by 50%. This was for the benefit of the people. The additional funds would be used to modernize the transportation system, which would benefit all the citizens of the capital. Already, many Party organizations, trade unions, spontaneous workers' meetings, schools, factories, institutes, and other organizations sent telegrams to the Central Committee of the Party expressing their full approval for the price increase. We had to do it too. He read the previously-prepared text of a telegram, which went like this:

> We, the teachers of School 98 in Bucharest, want to express our full agreement with the proposal of the Communist Party to raise the price of transportation in Bucharest by 50%. At the same time, we take this opportunity to thank the Communist Party and comrade Ceaușescu personally for his care for the welfare of the citizens of Romania. Comrade Ceaușescu, we pledge our determination to work harder for the fulfillment of all plans developed at the last congress of the Communist Party and to spare no effort to advance our country towards socialism and communism under your wise leadership.

As he was reading, I remembered two political jokes.

> On a bus in Bucharest, a lady suddenly announces that she is an official controller and will check if everybody has a ticket. All goes well, until she arrives at a man who says, "Sorry, I could not afford to buy a ticket. The Party is not paying me enough for food and transportation." The lady asks him for his identification papers and tells him he must pay a hundred Lei fine. Suddenly, another

225

man, nicely dressed, jumps in the conversation. "Comrade controller," he says, "I am a Securitate officer. This man has made a provocative statement. He comes with me." The lady controller defers to him. The Securitate officer grabs the man by his hand and forces him out at the first stop. The bus leaves. He turns to the poor man and says, "I am not with the Securitate;2 I did it to save you the fine. Go in peace."

The second one was told to me as something that really happened.

Late one cold and rainy winter evening, hundreds of people wait for the bus, which is forty-five minutes late. Everybody is upset and angry. The bus finally comes, and people scramble inside, but not all of them succeed. Some hang from the door, and the overcrowded bus can hardly move. Nobody talks inside the bus. Suddenly, a man shouts as loud as he can: "Long live the Communist Party! Long live comrade Nicolae Ceauşescu!" Everybody is petrified, as they understand this is a mockery. The man looks around and says, "Does anybody have any objection to that?"

After reading the text of the telegram, the principal said, "All in favor, raise your hands." All hands went up except mine, but nobody paid attention.

The principal turned towards the lady taking the minutes and told her: "Please record that the telegram was approved in unanimity."

I let it go. Once again, this was not my fight.

"Let's move to the second and final point of our meeting. The superior Party organization at the level of the Bucharest sector, as well as the sector school district, asked us to discuss the ways in which we can promote atheism among our students by using the subjects we teach in our school. As you know, atheist education is one of the important objectives given to us by the Communist Party, and an important responsibility for each one of us.

I have already asked three of our teachers to prepare a paper on this subject. Each one will refer to the subject that she teaches in our school. Comrade Ecaterina Popa, the biology teacher, will be first. Comrade Popa, please proceed."

The lady stood up and started to read from some sheets of paper. It was the usual stuff. In the ten minutes she was allocated, she managed to make a short mention that Darwin teaches us that there is no God. The rest was the wooden language we found on the first page of the Party newspaper, filled with empty phrases like, "Under the wise leadership of Comrade Nicolae Ceausescu, the most beloved son of the Romanian people..." or, "Comrade's Ceauşescu profound thinking is highly appreciated all over the world..." or, "As Comrade Nicolae Ceauşescu said at the 9th Congress of the Communist Party..." and so on and so forth.

Next, the history teacher proceeded in the same way. Somewhere between the usual phrases, she mentioned the Inquisition and Gordano Bruno, who was burnt at the stake as a martyr for science. It was, of course, all exaggerated and taken out of context.

Next came the math teacher.

This must be interesting, I thought. *How on earth will she link math with atheism?*

I felt sorry for her. I knew that the principal or the Party Secretary came to her and gave her the task to write a paper on the subject and to read it at the meeting. She reminded me of the nice ten-year-old girls I knew when I was in school, who were neat and clean, who always obeyed their parents and teachers, whose notebooks were always perfectly organized - not like mine, which tended to be messy - and who were always praised deservingly. I liked those girls; once I was even in love with one in the third grade. The math teacher who stood up to read her paper might have been a good mother and a good wife. She just did what she was told.

I listened with attention to her speech. The only link between math and atheism she mentioned was that we should use the concepts of derivatives and integrals to show children that there was no God.

When she finished, the Party Secretary asked if there was anybody who wanted to add anything to the main subject.

At that moment, I remembered an old friend, a Hungarian Christian called Pocsy. He worked for a school requisites company in the city of Oradea, where he was highly regarded due to his professionalism and good character. He told us how once they had a company-wide meeting in which, at the direction of the Communist Party, religion and atheism were discussed. The bottom line of what was said was that Christians are stupid. He stood up and said, "I am one of those stupid Christians," then sat down. Those few words invalidated everything that was said before.

It was now my time to act. Once, when I was a child, I denied God and my family's faith out of fear, and I still needed to redeem myself. So, I raised my hand. I think the Party Secretary was initially happy that there was a follow-up discussion; it would show well when her superiors read the minutes of the meeting.

I started.

"I've heard the three presentations on using our subjects in school to teach atheistic education. I can understand the examples of biology and history, although they are open for debate and much more can be said. However, as a math teacher myself, I cannot figure out how we can use math to teach atheism. The speaker mentioned the concepts of derivatives and integrals. There is no way I can use these math concepts to teach that there is no God.

There is, however, a remote connection. I can and indeed would like to tell my students that these concepts were introduced in mathematics by Isaac Newton. What I would also tell them is that the same genius who introduced these concepts, who discovered the law of gravity, and who made advances in optics, was at the same time a believer in God. Moreover, he was a theologian and he wrote a treaty on a book of the Bible, the book of Revelation."

229

I looked around. Next to me were seated some teachers who occupied strategic positions in which they could browse through magazines or write notes for their next class. Now they all stopped and looked at me. At the front table, the three people were looking at one another as if to say, "What do we do now?" I took advantage of their confusion and continued.

"On a related subject, this atheistic education is getting out of hand and prevents us from giving our students a solid education. If we read our Romanian literature classics, we find that they are filled with expressions from the Bible. Indeed, the whole European culture, of which we are a small part, is based on Christianity, on its morality, on its worldview, and on its Scriptures. By hiding the Bible from our students, we prevent them from understanding their own culture, their own heritage. I propose we introduce the Bible as a subject of study in our school."

That was too much. The Party secretary stood up and said, "Comrade Oara, sit down." Then she addressed the other participants, saying, "We do not have to listen to that," and then immediately changed the subject. The meeting had deviated from the predetermined scenario, and she did not want to continue the deviation.

When the meeting was over and we started to exit, some teachers avoided me, but others approached me and whispered, "Bravo, Oara. You said it so well!"

I went home that evening with the full expectation that I would soon be fired.

***

Two days after the meeting, the principal invited me to his office. He was almost laughing and seemed to be amused by the whole affair.

"Comrade Oara," he said, "the school district and the superior Party organization are aware of what happened in the meeting. I was asked to fire you. However, I want to give you a chance. Take advantage of the winter vacation and look for another job."

I loved him for that. He was one in a long series of people who were asked to harm me, but instead warned me and tried to protect me, while avoiding trouble at the same time.

I immediately started to look for a new job. I made many inquiries, but I found only two places that fit my profile.

One of the positions was at the Computer Center of the City of Bucharest, which today would we would call the IT Department. I had to go there and first take some tests. One was a generic intelligence test. Another was more specific, in which I had to design a computer algorithm to compute the day of the week for any date in the future. I had no problem with either of these tests.

A few days later, I received a phone call, and I was invited for an interview with the chief of the department. To my surprise, he was young, around thirty-five years old. We found that we had many common acquaintances, as we graduated from the same Faculty of Mathematics.. He told me that I got the highest scores they ever recorded for the tests, and that my hiring was virtually assured.

231

I waited a few days for a call from them, but nothing came. I waited more, then I called. A secretary told me that I was not accepted. I was disappointed and concluded that only my political file could have prevented them from hiring me.

I tried for the second position, a much more interesting one at the Institute for Petroleum Research. During the interview, I found out that they were working on the design of an oil rig in the Black Sea, and they needed a mathematician to work with the design team. For me, it was a dream job. I had studied mechanics in my last year, and I believed to be uniquely qualified for that position. As a top student at graduation, I should have had no reason to lose this opportunity.

After the interview, I started to dream about my new job. I loved applied mathematics because it always introduced new problems, from which new mathematical theories sprung. I would have a contribution to something tangible and of high value for our country, something that would generate billions in revenue and would insure the oil supply for Romania. Perhaps I would develop new directions in mathematics and publish articles in specialty magazines. Oil exploration was valued all over the world - maybe I would be invited to international conferences. It was more than I had ever expected. I started to think of withdrawing my application for emigration. I would have rather stayed to help my own country.

I waited again a few days, then I called the Institute. Nothing new. I called again, then again after a few days. Finally, a secretary told me that I was not accepted.

I understood at that moment that all doors were closed, and that I had no future in my own country. *Romania, I love you, I would have worked for you, I would have sacrificed for you, but I am rejected. Regretfully, I will have to leave.*

***

I returned to the school for the second trimester. The principal asked me one day how my job search was going, and I told him the truth: I had tried without success. He did not say anything, did not promise to keep me or press me to leave. I continued to work as a math teacher, trying to do a good job and enjoy it as much as possible.

I also continued my underground work, but at a slower pace. Moving from the center of the city to the periphery made it much more difficult for people to come and see me. Foreign visitors had a hard time finding my new residence in a sea of indistinct block of flats.

The high tide of dissident activities was receding. Father Gheorghe Calciu was arrested, and I knew little about his fate. Eventually, I found out that he was sentenced to ten years in prison. Paul Goma, who told the Securitate team accusing him of "unnatural relationships" that he had sex with Ceaușescu, went through an arrest and a long investigation, after which he was expelled from the country. The Free Workers Union leaders were arrested, some of those who signed to join the Union were given passports to leave the country, and the whole movement died.

I was able to send word to Father Calciu's wife that I could meet her at a precise place and time to hand her some money for her subsistence. The place was known in Bucharest as the Lion, as it was dominated by a large lion statue. I went there on a dark and rainy March evening, watching for any suspicious person and for any unusual movement. It looked like a spy movie, and I was tense and alert. I stayed partially hidden in some corner, so I was not visible, and hoped to see her coming. I waited about half an hour, but she did not come, so I went home.

In the spring, I was called to appear in front of a school district commission to discuss my application for emigration. It was a standard procedure: any organization where a passport applicant worked was supposed to attempt to dissuade him and convince him to withdraw his petition.

I showed up one afternoon at the school district building. I was invited to a room where four or five people were assembled, waiting for me. They were seated at one side of a table, and I sat opposite to them. They asked many questions, but I found two of them relevant and rational.

"Don't you love your country? You are well educated; why not use your talents and education here? Why would you give all that to America?"

"I love my country and I would like to serve her. Unfortunately, I cannot do that, as all my paths are blocked. I was told that, as a Christian, I cannot be a teacher. I tried applying for other jobs, but after some successful interviews, I was rejected. I am sure it was not because I was not capable, but because I am a Christian. How will I earn a leaving? Should I work as a manual laborer? If the

234

Communist Party is rejecting my offer to serve at my true capacity, I will go somewhere else, where I can use my talents. Every human is entitled to achieve his best. I cannot do so here, so I will have to go.

I desired all my life to be a mathematician. To pursue my dream, I would have to go for a PhD. However, the system in our country is such that one cannot start a PhD program without a recommendation from the Communist Party. Can you guarantee that I would receive such a recommendation? As Communists, would you recommend a Christian like me to enter a PhD program?"

They did not respond but moved to another question.

"The Romanian state paid for your education. You had a scholarship which covered tuition and expenses for all your years in college, not to mention the expense for your elementary and high school education. Don't you think that after all of this was offered to you for free, it would be unfair for you to just leave without giving anything back?"

"First," I responded, "I repeat that I am only leaving because I cannot work here at my capacity. How would I give back all that investment, which is substantial indeed? As a manual laborer in some factory? Isn't the state destroying my capacity to give back? Isn't the state and the Communist Party degrading everything that was invested in me?

There is, however, another aspect. How did the state pay for my education? Where did it get the money from? Was it not from the work of the common people? Was it not from the fruit of their labor and from the taxes they paid? Now consider this: my father has worked for over forty years. He lived a simple life, with no substantial material or financial rewards. Don't you think that in all those years of work he produced enough and paid enough taxes to cover his son's education? The Communist Party would have nothing if people like my father had not worked."

They listened and stayed quiet. They had a job to do, and they did it in a formal way. I think they believed me and had no stomach to engage in an argument. They would submit a report which showed that the meeting took place and that I was not persuaded.

I had no news about my application for a passport, and I was not going to inquire.

The Emigrant

Shortly after the end of the school year, I received a letter from the Passport Commission telling me that I could move to the next step of the process. I was invited to go to the Commission location to pick up my second set of forms for the passport. From everything I'd heard, at this point, the passport was approved in principle, although I would have to still go through several steps.

Besides the many forms I had to fill, there was also a long list of requirements, most of them having to do with the liquidation of my obligations to the Romanian state: taxes paid, electricity and gas payments up to date, no fees left to pay at the University, etc. The most important one was to return the apartment back to the city in good condition. I started to work through the list, checking all the obligations as fulfilled, one by one. I had to go and get papers and confirmations from all kinds of institutions, waiting in long lines, making phone calls, and arguing with obtuse bureaucrats. I had things to sell, things to give, and things to keep. This was not a trip, nor a move from one city to another, but the crossing of continents, cultures, and political and economic systems. If I left something important behind, I might not be able to recover it later.

In the beginning of September, I went to the school where I worked and resigned. It was difficult to continue my work there, as the preparation for departure was a full-time job. I met with Napoleon Ionescu, who was no longer the principal but a simple teacher I thanked him for his support and said goodbye. He shook my hand and wished me a good life in America.

It looked like smooth sailing to America, but more trouble was on the way. I called the local manager of the ICRAL, the city company responsible for the maintenance and administration of the city apartments. I told him that I needed a paper confirming that my apartment was in good condition and ready to be received back by his institution. It should not have been necessary, as after our departure Ana's sister and her family would continue to legally live in the apartment.

"I cannot simply give you a paper," he told me over the phone. "The apartment must be renovated and freshly painted before I give you the paper."

"Fine," I told him, "I'll take care of that."

We had a member of our church who was a skilled painter. He came and did exquisite work, such that the apartment looked better than ever, better than it must have been when brand new. I paid him around 2,000 lei for his work, which was the going price for painting an entire three-bedroom apartment.

I called the local ICRAL and told the manager that the apartment had been renovated.

"Can we get the paper now?" I asked.

"Slow down," he said. "I have to first come and inspect it." We made an appointment.

He showed up at our apartment after a few days with one of his subordinates. He was a handsome man, around forty, and looked like the French actor Alain Delon.

"As you can see," I said, "the apartment is already renovated and in excellent condition, without any blemish."

"That's not how it works," he said. "We cannot accept your amateurish renovation. We have to do it ourselves."

"But there is nothing else to be done," I protested. "You cannot add anything to the work which was already performed."

"Please do not teach me what is or is not to be done. We have our own rules. I cannot issue you the paper without showing that the proper renovation was executed by our state company."

"Does that mean that you'll send some workers here to repeat the work? That would be quite disrupting, not to mention the fact that in the end it would not look better."

"The actual work is not the point," he explained. "The point is that you must pay the fee for the renovation. When it would be performed is another matter. It may be soon, or even later, after you are gone."

"So, what is next?"

"We'll take some measurements and send you a bill to pay. After you pay the bill, everything will be in order and you will get your paper."

After about a week, I received a letter with a bill from ICRAL. My eyes popped. The bill was for 8,000 lei, four times what I paid for the same work. Besides, another renovation was not necessary anyway.

I went to the ICRAL manager's office and tried to reason with him, but he stood his ground, inflexible and unreasonable. Like any bureaucrat, he hid behind the supposed rules. I could not get the paper needed for the passport without paying the 8,000 Lei for the renovation. The problem was that I did not have that kind of money.

I tried to go over his head to his boss. I asked for an audience, and he received me one evening at another ICRAL location. I explained the whole issue. My way of seeing things was so obviously correct that it required little explanation.

"You have to pay the bill," the manager said.

"But the assessment is excessive," I protested.

"I trust my subordinate, he knows what he is doing. You must pay."

I was stuck and did not know what to do. I talked with several of my friends and asked for advice. Eventually, one of them smiled and told me, "Don't you understand what is happening? It's obvious. He expects a bribe."

I had never paid a bribe before. Is it correct? Is it moral? I decided that the moral burden was not on my shoulders. I was not bribing somebody to obtain an undeserved advantage. Rather, I was being extorted for my own rights. But how does one pay a bribe? What do I tell him when I give him the money? Should I look into his eyes? Should I wink? Should I smile?

I finally found the courage to do it. I pulled 2,000 lei from my diminishing reserves, put the money into an unsealed envelope, and went to the manager's office. The secretary opened the door to his room, I went inside, and he invited me to sit across the table from him. I was quite nervous.

"Regarding the paper I need for the passport," I said, "I believe we can find a satisfactory solution for all of us."

I pulled the envelope with the money from my pocket and placed it in front of him. I expected that he might explode in moral indignation. Instead, he was calm and smiled, as if to say, "I knew you'd give up and come to this." He took the envelope, opened it, counted the money, and then placed it in the drawer of his desk. He stood up, extended his hand to shake mine, and called his secretary.

"Please give Mister Oara his paper," he told her. To my surprise, the paper was ready and even signed by him. It confirmed that my apartment was in good condition and all my obligations were fulfilled.

I finally had all the papers in order, and one morning I went to the Passport Commission and submitted them at a window. I was hoping that the approval and the issue of the passports would come soon.

***

After two weeks, I received a call from the Passport Commission. Something was not in order with my papers, and I was invited to go there and discuss the issue with an official. He invited me to an office room, and we sat across a table. Another man was sitting next to him.

"There is a problem with your apartment," he told me. "Our documents show that your apartment is on Dimitrie Cantemir Boulevard, but all the papers you brought me refer to an apartment on Straja Street. You have to return to the state the apartment on the Dimitrie Cantemir Boulevard."

"I can understand why this mistake happened," I said. "We used to live on Dimitrie Cantemir, but about a year ago we moved to Straja. Your documentation is not up to date. You can check with the Sector City Hall and they will confirm that I now live at another address."

"That is not my job," he retorted, somehow annoyed. "I will not go chasing papers. Here it's written Dimitrie Cantemir Boulevard; this is what I need. You have to return this apartment to the state in order to get your passport."

"That would be impossible. It was an apartment switch, and now that apartment is occupied by another family. I cannot return to the state that which I do not have."

"This is your problem, not my problem. I am sure the switch was not done in a proper, legal manner."

"It was entirely legal." I said, "Therefore I cannot and should not be obliged to return that apartment."

The official sighed and turned to his colleague.

"I know what he did," he said, pointing at me. "He asked and got something like 50,000 Lei from that other guy. This is what these people do. The one with the larger or better apartment asks the other one to compensate him with cash in order to do the transaction. Nobody gives up a good apartment for a modest one. It is, however, illegal."

"He did not pay me anything," I jumped. "We did the switch out of necessity, not for a monetary gain." I proceeded to explain to him exactly what happened.

"Listen," he reacted, "you are not fooling me. You did something illegal and we caught you. Don't lie to my face."

"I did not receive any money, and the switch was performed with approval from the city. I have all the documents to prove that."

"I do not care about your documents. I'm sure the guy paid you. You must return the apartment on Dinitrie Cantemir if you want to get your passports. Anyway, you are taking up too much of my time. Go, and do not come back until you return the correct apartment to the state."

I thought for a few seconds.

"You surely understand my difficulty," I said. "How do you suggest I solve this problem?"

"This is your business. However, I suggest you ask the family in the old apartment to reverse the switch. If they do not agree, sue them."

"I have no basis to sue them, since the switch was legal. They waited for a long time to get an apartment in the center of Bucharest. They will not agree to reverse, and I cannot sue them."

He laughed. "Of course you cannot, after they paid you 50,000 Lei, which perhaps you have already spent or sent ahead of you to the United States by some illegal means."

He stood up, indicating that the discussion was over, and said, "Come back only when you are ready to return the apartment on Dimitrie Cantemir."

I left with no idea what I could do. I was stuck again, this time in a much worse situation than the previous one regarding the renovation of the apartment. It would have been unfair to sue Mr. Zidaru, who lived now with his family in my old apartment. He did not do anything wrong. Even if I did sue him, there was no chance I would win.

The next day, I went to the Bucharest Sector 4 building and asked to see the director of real estate administration. I had watertight logic: either the apartment switch was legal, in which case he should give me a paper confirming that, or it was not legal, in which case he should order a reverse of the switch. He listened to me, shrugged, and told me he would not do anything. I left without any progress.

There was only one more thing I could try: go the Bucharest City Hall and ask for an audience with the official in charge of all real estate in Bucharest. He had the power to solve my problem. If he did not, there was nothing else to do.

I called the City Hall, asked for an audience, and was scheduled to go there in a few days.

***

I went to the City Hall on a nice October morning, entered the building, found the office of the real estate director, and waited in an adjacent room. After about an hour, a lady secretary called my name and I went inside.

The director was a tall man and slightly overweight. He had a powerful position, controlling the living conditions of hundreds of thousands of families. Looking at his mean face, I felt like I had already lost.

I explained to him my situation and used my reasonable logic: either confirm that the apartment switch was legal (which it was!) or order to reverse it. I also told him that my request was related to my passport application.

"Are you one of the Jimmy Carter's Baptists?" he asked suddenly. He knew that Jimmy Carter was a Baptist and, in his mind, all Romanian Baptist were despicable traitors working for an American President. He also knew that there were other Baptists petitioning to leave the country.

"Yes, I am a Baptist, but I do not belong to Jimmy Carter and have nothing to do with him," I answered.

He cursed the Baptists, cursed Jimmy Carter, and cursed me.

"Go ask Jimmy Carter to solve your problem!" he shouted. "You people are traitors, sold to the Americans, and then you dare come here and beg for papers."

"But comrade director, all I want is ..."

He cursed me again.

"Get out of here, and I do not want to see your face ever again!" he shouted. "If you come again, I will call the police to arrest you for trespassing."

I went out, hearing him cursing again after me. I got out of the building, crossed the Boulevard, and entered the beautiful Cişmigiu Park, which was on the other side of the street.

I decided not to go directly home, but to walk through the park to cool my emotions and my head. I tried to take stock of my situation. What would happen next? I would not be able to return the old apartment, and the Passport Commission would not grant me the passports. My funds were running out, especially now that I did not have a job. I would not be able to gain employment, as any prospective employer would be told that I was a politically dangerous person, and besides, I was about to leave the country anyway. Ana would give birth in January to our second child, and, even if somehow the problem with the apartment was solved, I would have to refill the forms to include the second child. Even after that was done, I would not be able to leave immediately after the birth. In the meantime, I would have no money and no job. The Communist authorities would arrest me for parasitism, as they did in many other cases.

I was walking through the park alleys, looking at young couples holding hands or sitting on benches. Young mothers were walking slowly, pushing their babies in carriages. At some tables, older men were playing chess. Life went on in its charm and beauty, but I was in a deep and dark hole from which there was no way out.

> The enemy hath persecuted my soul; he hath smitten my life down to the ground; he hath made me to dwell in darkness, as those that have been long dead. Therefore is my spirit overwhelmed within me; my heart within me is desolate. I remember the days of old; I meditate on all thy works; I muse on the work of thy hands. I stretch forth my hands unto thee: my soul thirsteth after thee, as a thirsty land. Hear me speedily, O Lord: my spirit faileth: hide not thy face from me, lest I be like unto them that go down into the pit.

Psalm 143: 3-7

I ran out of all options. All that was left was to cry to God and pray.

Suddenly, I recognized a face in the crowd: it was Colonel Ștefănescu of the Securitate, who had interrogated me a little more than a year before. He was coming from the opposite direction, and we recognized each other.

"Hey, glad to see you, Oara," he said. He extended his hand, and we shook hands like old friends.

"Glad to see you too," I answered.

"So, how are you doing these days? If I remember correctly, we talked more than a year ago."

"I listened to your advice, and I applied for passports to emigrate to the United States."

"Do you already have passports?" he asked. Most likely, he already knew the answer but wanted to get somewhere with the conversation.

"Unfortunately, not yet," I answered.

"How come? Any problem?"

"Yes, as a matter of fact. The Passport Commission is asking me to return my old apartment, where another family now lives after an apartment switch. It is an absurd situation."

"And what are you going to do about it?"

"I just came out of the City Hall. I asked the real estate director to give me a paper showing that the switch was

248

entirely legal and that he expects me to return the new apartment to the state."

"And…?"

"He cursed me and threw me out of his office."

He shook his head in apparent disbelief.

"I can't believe it," he said, "but maybe we can help."

"I am sure you can help," I said, "and I would be grateful to you if you did."

"Sure, sure. But first I would like to ask you a few questions."

At that point, I became suspicious. The Securitate was not in the compassion business. They would not do something for free.

"Last week," he said, "you met a British citizen in a hotel. I'd like to know why and what you discussed."

It was true; I had met Alan, an old friend, who worked with the Center for the Study of Religion and Communism in the U.K. He sent me word through a common acquaintance to come to his hotel at a precise time on a certain day. I went directly to the elevator without talking to anybody at reception, and I took it to to his floor. I did not see anybody on the corridor, and quite hoped the meeting would pass unobserved. When I knocked, he opened the door and put his finger to his lips, indicating

249

that we should not speak yet. Then he took me to the bathroom, where he turned all the faucets on. If any secret microphones were there, the noise of the water was supposed to cover our voices, as we only talked in whispers. I gave him news about some new cases of harassment of Christians, and we talked about the dissidents who were watched by the authorities. I finally left, getting out of the hotel as soon as I could, without raising any suspicion.

I had no idea how the Securitate knew about the meeting. Somebody on their side must have watched the lobby and inconspicuously taken pictures of the people coming and going. The Securitate already knew my face, so it was not difficult for them to put things together.

"You know, he is a British spy," added the colonel.

"Oh," I said, surprised. "I was not aware of that."

"Of course, of course. How do you know him?"

"He used to visit our church often when he was student in Bucharest. I believe he was studying our language and took some courses at the Orthodox seminary. He used to come to our youth meetings, and when we sang he would accompany us on his guitar."

I was volunteering to tell him as much as I could about things he already knew.

"How did you know where and when to meet him?"

"Oh, that was strange. A person totally unknown to me approached me after church and told me that Alan would like to see me, and he told me when and where. I would not have listened to a stranger, but since I knew it was Alan, I decided to go."

The colonel shook his head. He did not believe me, and he knew I was aware of that, but he continued with his questions.

"What did you discuss?"

"Usual stuff: church, faith, old friends. He asked me how Pastor Taloş was doing."

"I believe you discussed much more than that."

"Oh, yes, I remember. He also passed to me greetings from my father-in-law in America."

"You should be careful, Oara, otherwise you will end up receiving greetings in prison."

"I hope that would never happen," I said.

He seemed to give up. Disappointingly for him, I had not changed, and my desperate situation was not enough to make me more malleable.

"Very well, let's get back to your passport. Who was the idiot at the City Hall who refused your request?"

I was surprised and amused to hear him calling that high official an idiot, but, after all, the Securitate was the highest power in the state, apart from the Communist Party. I gave him the name. He pulled a small notebook from his pocket and wrote it down.

"This is what you do," he said. Go back there tomorrow at nine in the morning. Ask again for the paper, and this time you will receive it."

"Thank you, comrade Colonel," I said, this time with real sincerity.

We shook hands and departed. It was the last time in my life I met Colonel Ștefănescu.

***

I went again to the City Hall the next morning and asked the secretary to let me speak again with her boss. I was pushing my luck, as I did not have an appointment, and besides I had been threatened to never show up there again.

"What is your name?" the secretary asked. "Oh, you do not have to go inside. I already have your paper here, signed by the boss." The paper confirmed - this time with the signature of a high official - that the apartment switch we had made was entirely legal and that the city now expected me to turn over the space in my current apartment upon my departure.

The Securitate was efficient, indeed. All my respect for them!

I picked up the much-desired paper and took it to the Passport Commission the same day. I did not receive any more objections about the apartment. Perhaps they knew all along what was right, but somehow the Securitate wanted to use the whole affair to try once again to break me.

***

I received a call shortly thereafter to go pick up my passports. I went to the Commission building, and a lady at a window handed me the passports. I was glad to see they were green passports, which meant I was retaining my Romanian citizenship. Other people received brown passports, which allowed them to travel out of the country, but without citizenship. They could not legally return. One such case was of the pastor Liviu Olah. He went to the United States and tried to enroll in a theological school, saying that his goal was to return and continue his ministry in Romania. When they saw his passport, without citizenship, they cut his stipend and he could not continue.

When I came out of the building, I had the last episode in which the Securitate tried to ensnare me. A man of around forty ran after me and asked in an agitated voice, "Did you get a passport to leave the country?"

"Yes, I did," I answered.

"Me too. I waited years to get it. These guys are wicked," he said, after which he cursed the Communist Party. "Where are you going first?"

"Most probably Rome," I said.

253

"I'm going there too. Look, I think we should organize. Once we are there we can start a protest movement, demonstrate in front of the Romanian Embassy, and get in touch with people back here who want to fight the Communist regime."

It was a crude provocation. No serious dissident would curse the Party in the street and propose a political fight to a stranger. He was either silly and unbalanced, or an agent provocateur. I was sure it was the latter rather than the former.

"I am not interested," I answered shortly, turning my back to leave.

I do not think the provocation was organized by my nemesis, Colonel Ştefănescu; he would have been more sophisticated. I rather believe it was some trap set by another section of the Securitate, a kind of fishing expedition to catch some sufficiently naïve people.

It was now November, and we started to prepare for our exit. Having the passports was not enough: I had to get visas to enter another country. I knew I would be admitted to the United States, as the American Vice Consul had already told me so, even before I was thinking about leaving. However, it was more complicated than getting a visa from the American Consulate. There was no basis for direct admission to the United States. On my Romanian application I had indicated "family reunification" as the reason for my request, but the United States did not recognize this, as Ana was an adult, married with a child, and could not claim reunification with her former family. The United States could admit us as political refugees, but we were not refugees, as we were still residing in our own country. There was, however, a nice trick. The American Consulate gave us a paper indicating that if we arrived in Italy, they would guarantee we'd receive visas for the United States. I took the paper to the Italian Consulate, which, based on the American assurance, gave us visas for Italy.

The American Consulate also took care of our accommodations in Rome. We were passed to an international charity, the Tolstoy Foundation, which had a representative at the Consulate. They made all the arrangements, telling us that somebody would wait for us at the airport in Rome. We would have a place to stay and food to eat. All expenses were covered by the Tolstoy Foundation.

***

Our last week in Romania, at the end of November, was frantic. We scrambled to get all we needed for the move to America. We had to choose what to take and what to leave behind. We met many friends and said goodbye, thinking that some we would never see again. We had an emotional last day at our church. People came and embraced us, some with tears in their eyes.

My parents and my sister arrived from Alba Iulia to stay with us those last days and accompany us at the airport. By a strange coincidence, my father retired a few days before our departure, after more than forty years of work. His life would change dramatically, and he would miss his son, daughter-in-law, and grandson.

We left Bucharest on the 30th of November 1980, one day before the 58th anniversary of the Union of Transylvania and Romania, which would later become the national day of Romania. We were accompanied to the airport by many friends. We hugged and kissed, but I paid special attention to my parents. When would they see us again? In five years? In ten years? Maybe never.

A last hug, then we went through passport control and security, then a last look back, a wave, and we were gone. As we were waiting at the gate, Ruben, our nearly two-year-old son, looked in amazement at the planes on the tarmac, pointing to each one and shouting, "The plane, the plane." It was an early sign, as in twenty-five years he would become first a United States Air Force pilot, then a commercial airline pilot.

After the plane took off for Rome, Ana fell asleep, exhausted from a whole night of packing and an emotional departure. I held Ruben and my thoughts moved back and forth between the past and the future. I remembered an old Romanian proverb: An hour can bring more than a whole year.

The Immigrant

As we disembarked in Rome and then were taken by a minibus to the Pensione Ortensia, near Stazione Termini, the main train station in Rome, we were shocked by the vivid colors and the streets bursting with life. When we left, Bucharest was bleak, colorless, and cold. We were absorbing every new aspect of life which was unfamiliar and enchanting.

In Rome, our room and meals were paid by the Tolstoy Organization, which helped emigrants from Eastern Europe. We had only $100 to spend on other things, but we had youth and hope on our side. We visited as many monuments as was possible. The museums – where one had to pay – were less accessible. I was delighted to see the Column of Trajan, still standing after 1,900 years, on which the whole story of the Roman conquest of Dacia was recorded in bas-reliefs.

On December 9, we went to the airport to embark on the Pan Am flight to New York. As we entered the plane, we received copies of various newspapers, including *The New York Times*. The cover had some sensational news: John Lennon was shot and killed near Central Park in New York. At the first glance, I did not know it was THE John Lennon of the Beatles, so I thought, "How strange, this man who was killed had the same name as the famous Beatles singer." It was only when I started to read that I realized it was the real John Lennon.

Disembarking in New York, I had my first language blunder in my new country. I left Ana and Ruben behind and passed security to see if my in-laws arrived to pick us up, but they were not yet there. Returning to Ana, a policeman stepped towards me and challenged me: "May I help you?" I thought, "How nice that this policeman wants to help me," so I smiled and said, "No, thank you," then continued to walk past security. Surprised, he ran after me and stopped me, explaining that I was not allowed to pass in that direction. Now I was in a difficult situation. Ana was waiting with Ruben and all our luggage inside, but I could not go and pick them up. I explained the situation to the policeman, who understood and let me pass, perhaps contrary to the regulations.

We had a great meeting with my in-laws. My father-in-law was now the pastor of the Romanian Baptist Church in Queens. As we had our first meal together, many other people from the church came to meet us.

My father-in-law had rented an apartment for us right next to the church. It was a one-bedroom apartment, otherwise large and clean, and completely furnished. It was bliss!

The next day, my brother-in-law Andrei took me to Princeton, where Richard Wurmbrandt, the famous Romanian Jew who converted to Christianity, was going to speak in a church. In Romania, he had spent fourteen years in prison, where he was often close to death. After he was allowed to emigrate, he wrote a couple of books, including *Tortured for Christ*. He was a real legend among Evangelical Christians in Romania and perhaps in the West.

In Princeton, I had a weird encounter. I was walking on a street close to the University, when I passed a person I thought I recognized as my former assistant professor of algebra, Dorin Popescu. *That is impossible*, I thought, and walked past him. However, I turned my head for a second look, and he did the same, and we recognized each other. We shook hands and talked. He told me he was at Princeton's Institute for Advanced Studies, where he had won a fellowship. This time, we could openly discuss our political opinions and impressions about what was happening in Romania. He said he intended to return there, whatever happened.

My second son, David, was born in a hospital in Queens on January 8, 1981. Now I had a wife, two sons, no job, and no way to support my family.

Over the next months, I struggled to achieve two objectives: enroll in a PhD program at a prestigious American university, and at the same time get a job. The first goal was not too difficult, and I was accepted for a PhD in Mathematics at the Courant Institute at New York University. However, after two years in which I took one course per semester (my job and family did not allow for more), I abandoned the program. The main reason was that, by that time, I was reorienting myself to a software engineering position in New York, where there were plenty of opportunities and good pay, which I needed for my family. The final decision to abandon was when I saw posters at the university announcing jobs for fresh PhDs at half the salary I was already making. My old dreams were coming into contradiction with the new realities of life. I chose family over a career in mathematics.

Finding a job proved to be much more difficult. I was facing the same chicken and egg problem which most fresh graduates face: the requirement for almost any job was experience, but experience could only be acquired with a job. I sent my resume to tens, if not hundreds, of places, with no results. I lowered my demands for a salary to a low minimum, perhaps not knowing that this in itself communicated a lack of confidence.

It was one of my lowest moments in life. Only months before, I was a recognized leader among Evangelical Christians and many people were coming to talk with me. I was involved in secret operations related to forbidden materials and I lived a life of constant danger. The Securitate paid attention to me, followed me, and listened to my phone calls. I was, in other words, at the center of attention and my life was significant for myself and those around me.

Now I was alone, except my immediate family. Nobody was hostile to me, but nobody cared about who I was. My life was becoming utterly insignificant and devoid of meaning. Those were my feelings anyway, as I knew that theologically every life is significant, at least to God and to the family.

I had no choice but to apply first for food stamps and then for public assistance, which was neither my intention nor my expectation when I came to America. Every month, I had to visit the food stamps office to renew my application.

At that time, something comical happened. I was notified by an official letter that to receive public assistance, I had to present myself to a center where my skills were to be tested so that perhaps I could be placed into a job. Of course, I had to go.

A lady at the office told me that I must take two tests: one for my English skills, and one for my math skills. The math required was at the middle school level, so I told the lady that the math test was unnecessary, as I was already involved in a postgraduate mathematics program at New York University. She was unmoved by my argument and told me in a dry voice that, if I want to receive public assistance, I must take the test. I did, and I found myself again doing additions and multiplications. Fortunately, I passed. The English test was less trivial, but, after the results were verified, a lady informed me that I had the best score in my group of about 30 people.

I grew more and more desperate in my job search. Ana's family helped us as much as they could, but it was unfair to them to support us with their modest resources. I felt worthless and lost. Walking on the streets, I looked with envy at the truck drivers who had jobs, at the store clerks who had jobs, at the people rushing to offices in the morning. I was looking at the tall buildings in Manhattan, where multitudes worked every day, able to support their families. There were tens of thousands, maybe hundred of thousands who worked as programmers, something I could very well do. *Please, give me a chance*, I felt like shouting. *I am a young and capable man, I can work like a horse and you will be happy you hired me.*

As I sent my resumé to many places and knocked on many doors without success, I decided to make two corrections. The first was to stop lowering my announced salary expectations. I remembered how once, back at home in Romania, when I tried to make some money tutoring in math, I got more demand when I announced a high price per class. Yes, people thought they were hiring a more valuable teacher (which was only partially true, as I was not necessarily a good tutor.)

The second adjustment was to "enhance" my resumé. Initially I had some moral problems with it, which I quickly overcame, mostly out of necessity. I remembered the words of the Apostle Paul, "The one who does not provide for his family is worse than an infidel." That seemed a much greater offence than a white lie. Even so, I would have not done it except that I also put into practice the same theory of truth which I used in my clashes with the Securitate. There was a difference between the incidental and mechanical truth and the essential truth, the same as between a photograph of Mona Lisa's hand and the portrait painted by Leonardo. One is very exact but does not tell too much. The other is imprecise but tells much more about the lady. Translated to my case, here was the difference: if I stated that I was a Romanian graduate with no experience, everybody would think that I was a low-quality worker who would take a lot of time to become productive. Most people did not know that Romania had a very powerful and internationally recognized math school and did not know that we had high-quality education. (Incidentally, I found later that most Romanian immigrant children who were tested at arrival were placed in grades superior to that of their age.) However, if I claimed some IT experience, my chances would improve.

One thing I remembered from my interrogation days was that when one makes statements which do not reflect the perfect truth, he or she tends to be vague, and, to overcome that, one has to come up with many vivid details.

262

That was easy for me. I interviewed once for a position with the Bucharest Computer Center, but was rejected for political reasons. I could repeat the interview in great detail, and just change the outcome. Once hired by the Bucharest Computer Center, I worked on a bunch of interesting and challenging projects (at least in my imagination). I included the names of the projects in my resume and was prepared to give more details. I knew that no prospective employer in New York would call Bucharest to verify my resume claims.

With my enhanced credentials, I finally got my first interview in May of 1981, at Chase Manhattan Bank. I was interviewed by two managers, a lady and a man. I did very well with the lady, but I still believe she wanted to hire me more out of motherly compassion than out of trust. With the man, it was different. He was a Hungarian Jew and knew more about the state of IT in Eastern Europe than I expected. Some of his questions took me to some delicate territory, and I believe he felt my unease. However, he noticed that I was not so dumb, and I suppose he felt some solidarity with a fellow East European. I was fortunate to get an offer after a few days, with a relatively low salary but much better than I expected. Now I could feed my family, even take them to a McDonald's occasionally, and pay with my own money. That sounded quite pathetic for a former anti-Communist fighter, but I had to take whatever life offered.

I realized that I was like a young tree, taken from its original ground. Initially, the leaves wither and fall and the branches start to bend. Planted in a new ground, it slowly comes back to life.

Epilogue

Ceausescu fell in December 1989, ten years after I left Romania. He and his wife were hated by the great majority of Romanians for the hunger, for the lies and humiliations they had to endure. Only three years before that, Elena Ceaușescu had ordered the demolition of a most-revered church, the 800-year-old church of Saint Parascheva, People gathered around the church and tried to protect it. The police intervened and arrested many of the protesters and moved the crowd away. The workers brought to perform the demolition refused to do it. Authorities brought common criminals from prisons and promised them reduced time for doing the job. One of them climbed to take out the church bell and fell to his death.

When revolution broke in Bucharest, Ceaușescu ordered the troops to come into the city and fire on the protesters. Many were killed, including students who were massacred in the University Square next to the building where I attended courses. Eventually, the army turned, and Ceaușescu and his hated wife had to flee. They were caught and later executed on Christmas Day. Watching the developments from the United States, we rejoiced initially, but later realized it was done for dark reasons. If they were put on trial, many other people from the second echelon of the Communist Party would have been exposed as collaborators. As it happened, this second echelon acquired the power, at least for a few years until they were voted out. Romania joined NATO and later the European Union.

Antonie Iorgovan, the former leader of the Communist Students' Association at the University of Bucharest, who promised to personally ensure my expulsion from the University, had a stellar career after the Romanian Revolution of December 1989. The country needed a new constitution, so the man who once told me that the constitution was sufficiently elastic and could mean whatever he wanted became the chief of the state commission entrusted to create a new one. He became a senator, and in fact I liked some of his positions. In 2005, he was diagnosed with pancreatic cancer and received treatment at some of the best hospitals in Europe but died soon after.

My biology teacher, who used to mock the "stupid Christians" during his classes, died while I was still a student in Bucharest. He went to visit a relative in the mountains, got drunk one night, fell into a river and drowned.

I do not know what happened to the Securitate officers who interrogated me. After the revolution, the Securitate was disbanded and was replaced with the Romanian Information Service. Most former officers were forced to retire. Do not feel sorry for them. Many became rich by exploiting the skills, contacts, and knowledge about society and economy which they had acquired under the Communist regime.

I do not harbor any grudges against the people who interrogated me; they were just doing their job. In the 1950s, there were many sociopaths or psychopaths in the Securitate, but, by the 1970s, when I had my clashes with them, things were different. Moreover, at the time of the Romanian Revolution in December 1989, most Securitate officers were aware that the country was sliding towards an abyss under Ceausescu and wanted him gone.

I found out a few years ago that it is now possible for a Romanian citizen to view his own Securitate file. Some of my friends have done it and had the unpleasant experience of finding that some of their acquittances had informed on them. Maybe I will see my file one day and will discover the same, but I already know I will not judge or despise the people who informed on me. Most of them were themselves victims of the system. The only ones who should be ashamed are those who used their position as informers to take revenge against a neighbor, or those who did it out of malice or greed.

Some good things happened to the people who were a blessing in my life.

Vasile Tonoiu, who risked his career by refusing to fail me in his philosophy class, was kept as lecturer during the Communist years, but became full professor after the revolution, and eventually became a member of the Romanian Academy.

Professor Nicolae Cristescu came to the United States and became full professor of mechanics at the University of Florida.

Pavel Niculescu, who was so hurt when the regime had him expelled just before graduation from Orthodox seminary, came to New York, completed his studies, and got a PhD in Theology.

Father Calciu was sentenced to ten years in prison, but was eventually released after the intervention of many world leaders. He was allowed to come to the United States with his family. This extraordinary man worked for a while as a manual laborer, and later was reinstated as a priest in a Romanian Orthodox Church in Alexandria, Virginia. I once had the joy of visiting him in his new parish. Later, he became sick with cancer. He visited his country one more time, then returned to U.S. and died here.

My father-in-law was the pastor of the First Romanian Baptist Church in New York for a few years, and later retired in Portland, Oregon, where most of his children and over thirty grandchildren live now. He died in 2012.

My dream of becoming a mathematician did not come to pass. I liked what I was doing as a software developer, and, besides, I discovered that software, in many of its aspects, was not too far from mathematics. I found my niche in areas of software which were highly mathematical: complex algorithms, optimization, and compilers. In 1987, I had the satisfaction to use real math, when a large investment firm in New York asked me to develop a method to optimize portfolios of hedge funds to minimize risk. I still like to pick up interesting math problems and attempt to solve them. I dream that I will continue this in heaven - not as a researcher, but as one who would contemplate beautiful mathematical structures. As mathematics reflects God's truth, by knowing God more, I will be able to understand and admire the beauty which emanates from the Creator.

In 2000, Ana and I went back to the Orthodox Church, bringing three of our children with us. My parents and Ana's parents lived the first part of their lives as Orthodox, the second as Baptists. We did that in reverse, growing up as Baptist and then turning Orthodox, completing the whole cycle. On the other hand, both our parents and we moved from a majority to a minority. They were Evangelicals in a country with an Orthodox majority; we became Orthodox in a country with an Evangelical majority.

Looking back, I can see how lucky I was. Maybe I should say "blessed," but the great blessing is for those who really suffered. Maybe God knew I was weak, so He only allowed some easy trials for me. Some other people, like Father Gheorghe Calciu, Father Nicolae Steinhardt, Father Roman, and Richard Wurmbrandt, were much stronger, and they endured years of prison and torture. To them, "Blessed are the persecuted" applies. They are my true heroes.